SECOND EDITION

How to Pass

HIGHER

English

Ann Bridges
Consultant editor: Carolyn Cunningham

HODDER
GIBSON
AN HACHETTE UK COMPANY

The Publishers would like to thank the following for permission to reproduce copyright material.

Photo credits

p.13 © Ingo Bartussek – Fotolia; **p.21** The Kiss by Gustav Klimt © PAINTING / Alamy; **p.45** © Stockbyte/Photolibrary Group Ltd; **p.75** © Leon Neal/Getty Images; **p.125** © Mander and Mitchenson/University of Bristol/ArenaPAL; **p.145** © Stockbyte/Getty Images; **p.151** © MarkaBond/Fotolia.com; **p.156** © Bazmark Films/Warner Bros./Kobal/REX/Shutterstock.

The author and publishers would like to thank the staff and students of Madras College for the use of the photos on pages 161, 162 and 163.

Acknowledgements

Please see page 170.

Every effort has been made to trace all copyright holders, but if any have been inadvertently overlooked, the Publishers will be pleased to make the necessary arrangements at the first opportunity.

Although every effort has been made to ensure that website addresses are correct at time of going to press, Hodder Gibson cannot be held responsible for the content of any website mentioned in this book. It is sometimes possible to find a relocated web page by typing in the address of the home page for a website in the URL window of your browser.

Hachette UK's policy is to use papers that are natural, renewable and recyclable products and made from wood grown in well-managed forests and other controlled sources. The logging and manufacturing processes are expected to conform to the environmental regulations of the country of origin.

Orders: please contact Bookpoint Ltd, 130 Park Drive, Milton Park, Abingdon, Oxon OX14 4SE. Telephone: (44) 01235 827827. Fax: (44) 01235 400454. Email: education@bookpoint.co.uk Lines are open from 9 a.m. to 5 p.m., Monday to Friday, with a 24-hour message answering service. Visit our website at www.hoddereducation.co.uk. If you have queries or questions that aren't about an order, you can contact us at hoddergibson@hodder.co.uk

© Ann Bridges 2019
First published in 2019 by
Hodder Gibson, an imprint of Hodder Education
An Hachette UK Company
211 St Vincent Street
Glasgow, G2 5QY

Impression number	5	4	3
Year	2022	2021	2020

All rights reserved. Apart from any use permitted under UK copyright law, no part of this publication may be reproduced or transmitted in any form or by any means, electronic or mechanical, including photocopying and recording, or held within any information storage and retrieval system, without permission in writing from the publisher or under licence from the Copyright Licensing Agency Limited. Further details of such licences (for reprographic reproduction) may be obtained from the Copyright Licensing Agency Limited, www.cla.co.uk

Cover photo © abstract412/123RF.com
Illustrations by Barking Dog Art Design & Illustration
Typeset in Cronus Pro Light 13/15pt by Aptara, Inc.
Printed in India
A catalogue record for this title is available from the British Library.
ISBN: 978 1510 452244

MIX
Paper from
responsible sources
FSC™ C104740
www.fsc.org

SCOTLAND
EXCEL

We are an approved supplier on the Scotland Excel framework.

Schools can find us on their procurement system as:
Hodder & Stoughton Limited t/a Hodder Gibson.

Contents

Introduction

The aim of this book is, obviously, to help you to pass Higher English. That's what it says on the tin –and that is what, for the most part, it does. Where the book diverges from that aim, and it does sometimes, it moves on to become a book that might be entitled 'How to Pass Higher English Well'.

There is basic information on all aspects of the examination – from little things like semi-colons to big things like Shakespeare's plays – but there are also advanced hints and advice for those of you who want to get a really good result – after all, this is Curriculum for Excellence.

You will also find that there is a lot of cross-referencing. What you learn about writing discursive essays, for example, is reinforced by what you learn about understanding and analysing non-fiction texts in the next part of the book. And what you learn in the Understanding, Analysis and Evaluation section helps you to answer the questions on specified Scottish texts. These skills are also needed for writing your Critical Essay. And, finally, your ability to understand, analyse and evaluate your literary texts can be applied to your own writing for the folio – so we are back where we started. Nothing in an English course is wasted! That is why it is quite important to read **all** sections of the book – not just the ones you think apply to you. The skills in English are interdependent: the difference from task to task is merely in how you apply them.

There is a mixture of all the following methods: direct teaching; hints about possible misunderstandings and mistakes; sample questions; exercises to allow you to try out what you have just learned. There are summaries which suggest what you should have learned. But, most importantly, there are **sample answers**. You can use these to check your own attempts against an example of a 'good' answer, or you can 'cheat' and look up the answer before you try to answer the question. It doesn't really matter how you use them, so long as you take time to carefully read the answers **and** the advice which follows many of them. There is probably as much 'teaching' in the commentaries on the answers as there is in the body of the book, so spending time on them is really worthwhile.

You may find some of the vocabulary used in this book hard; some of the questions and exercises will certainly be too hard at the beginning of your Higher year. Most of the answers provide far more than you would be expected to write, but they are meant to cover a variety of possibilities. As you know by now, there is no such thing as the one and only 'correct' answer to questions on English texts. It's also important to remember that teaching has limited value unless accompanied by your active engagement. All the components of this book provide resources for your learning and for the enhancing of your potential as an English student.

What you should know

The exam has two papers: Reading for Understanding, Analysis and Evaluation (30 marks), and Critical Reading (40 marks). There are two additional elements (the Portfolio–writing, and Performance–spoken language) that are not done in the exam. You are given time throughout the year to work on the folio, and to demonstrate your skills in spoken language. Once your folio of writing is completed, your teacher will send it to the SQA to be marked (30 marks). Your teacher will assess your skills in spoken language. There are no marks or grades for this element: it is assessed 'achieved', or 'not achieved'.

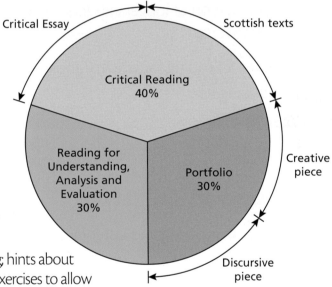

How the marks add up:

- Reading for Understanding, Analysis and Evaluation – 30 marks
- Critical Reading – 40 marks
  - Critical Essay – 20 marks
  - Scottish texts – 20 marks
- Portfolio – 30 marks
  - Creative piece – 15 marks
  - Discursive piece – 15 marks
- Performance–spoken language – achieved/not achieved (0 marks)

Chapter 1
Folio of writing

As the folio of writing is the first finished product that you have to generate as part of your external examination for Higher English, we will look at this first.

You have two essays to produce: one broadly 'discursive' and the other broadly 'creative'. Each is marked out of 15. You have a considerable amount of time to prepare and produce what will count for 30 per cent of your marks, so make a start in advance and don't leave anything till the last minute!

How you work on your folio and the deadlines you have to meet will be controlled by your centre; your teacher will give you this information.

This part of your exam attainment is the one that is most within your control. It is probable that, given time and effort on your part and with appropriate support, you can write two essays of Higher standard. The advice that follows is designed to help you in the process, but it goes further than that. There are tips here to help you aim for a very good result. Some of the advice is quite detailed, especially towards the end of the section – but extra marks are valuable and you can gain them in your own time without being under pressure in the exam hall.

The process of your writing may be monitored in a variety of ways, and as a result of varying teaching contexts, but your topic and your draft will be overseen. You should use feedback advice given by your teacher or lecturer in your final version and also make sure that you are acknowledging all your sources. You must avoid plagiarism. There is a document about what this means on the SQA website, so that there is no excuse for not adhering to the conditions.

Hints & tips

The number of marks available for your folio (30) is the same as the number of marks available for the Reading for Understanding, Analysis and Evaluation exam paper (30), which you will sit in May. So it makes sense to make a good effort in writing.

The technicalities – the easier part

1 Each essay should be accurate in its use of language – punctuation, sentencing, spelling and capitalisation should all be correct. Because this is not an exam setting, you have plenty of time to go over your work with a fine toothcomb and with a dictionary. Remember that you are allowed to use such tools as dictionaries and a spellchecker. But beware of accepting blindly what a spellcheck program suggests – sometimes it will give an alternative that is not quite what you meant. Remember also that it cannot distinguish between such things as the correct/ incorrect use of *its/it's*, *their/there/they're*, etc., so you'll need to pay special attention to these.

2 Your essays should be within the specified word limit – 1,300 words. Going over the word limit is risky: this can affect the structure and

Remember

These three technical items are always within your control.

effectiveness of the piece. An essay that is too long may not end up achieving as good a mark as a more concise text within the word limit.

3 Your essays must be completed by the correct date.

Hints & tips

SQA's definition of technical accuracy for folio pieces is as follows:

Few errors are present: paragraphs, sentences and punctuation are mostly accurate and organised so that the writing is clearly and readily understood; spelling errors (particularly of high frequency words) are infrequent.

No matter how good the content, story, argument, etc., consistent technical accuracy is a requirement for the piece to meet the minimum requirements for the 9–7 band.

Technical accuracy is an equally important requirement for the Critical Essay in the Critical Reading paper (see page 134).

The content – the more difficult part

Your writing at Higher level must be appropriate for purpose and audience, follow a line of thought based on relevant research/experience/ knowledge of genre, and be expressed in language appropriate to convey clearly thought/argument (on topics normally of a complex nature)/ emotions/concerns. Add to that some of the keywords that typify what is needed to achieve high marks:

- strong degree of mature reflection
- insight
- sensitivity
- skilful command of the genre
- thematic concerns which are skilfully introduced and developed
- strong impact.

Your essay(s) should be informed and relevant for your audience – that involves, in some cases, the collection and organisation of your data/ material/ideas; in other cases it involves the exercise of the imagination and the capturing of feelings and emotions.

One piece of writing must be what is classed as broadly 'discursive'. This will be one of:

- an argumentative essay
- a persuasive essay
- a report
- an informational piece.

The other piece of writing must be what is classed as broadly 'creative'. This will be one of:

- a personal essay
- a reflective essay
- an imaginative piece.

Discursive essays

When marking your essay, examiners are assessing it as 'broadly discursive', which means they are not worried about the strict definition of your essay as either argumentative or persuasive. In fact, as you will see over the following pages, these two styles of writing share several common features. It can, however, be valuable to you when starting your essay to think of it as taking either an argumentative or persuasive approach, and the guidance below is intended to help you with this.

In this section, advice will also be given on reports, as well as informative writing. These types of essay can sometimes be referred to as 'transactional' and you may find, as with similarities between argumentative and persuasive, that there are several elements in common here too.

Argumentative essay

This kind of essay follows an 'argument' – not in the sense that you may have a row with a friend, but in the way that you have come to understand the meaning of the word in your Critical Essay work. The 'argument' of a play or a poem is really the thought process that involves the audience/reader in increasing their understanding of the play or poem.

In an argumentative essay, therefore, the exploration of a particular topic should have as its purpose the wish to inform, expand and clarify the reader's thoughts.

The important word here is 'exploration'. When you set out to write on a topic that interests you, you will already have some ideas about it. But probably your information is fairly superficial – perhaps a chance television programme, or a family discussion, or a topic touched on in class. You need to explore the ideas further, and then to guide your reader through these ideas.

Very occasionally, you may be such an expert in your field that you do not feel the need to do any research – say you come from a family of farmers, and have discussed endlessly some of the issues associated with the Common Agricultural Policy. Be aware that perhaps your (and your family's) views might be biased. The same reasoning applies to those of you whose family consists of tree surgeons, teachers or taxi drivers. Generally, essays written off the top of your head may be interesting, but will lack substance.

Several topics may have been suggested to you in the course of your studies, and discussed in class, but you still need to do your own research, and present your own ideas and conclusions.

Research

This is the first tool of writers of non-fiction – biographers, essayists, historians, social commentators and newspaper reporters to name but a few. And that now includes you.

As with all research, you may find that your original ideas about your topic are wrong, or only partially proven, or too cut-and-dried. This is one of the values of research – if you have a truly open mind you may have to change it!

Hints & tips

Make a note of *every* single book, article, site, etc. you consult *as you read it*. Although you may only use a fraction of what you read, you must be able to put the references for what you do use in your bibliography.

The research tools at the call of a modern writer are truly amazing. With a click of a mouse, or the touch of a screen, a mass of material is available. But that advantage can also be a disadvantage. If there is too much information, where do you start? Your training should enable you to go to reputable sites, back catalogues of 'serious' newspapers, books (check the writers' credentials), downloads of documentaries from reliable sources (which does not include everything on YouTube).

Research is betrayed as shallow when a bibliography records only one article from a tabloid newspaper and a reference to Wikipedia – although Wikipedia can be useful and can provide a good starting place for deeper research.

You can also use interviews and oral material, but you must record your sources.

Statistics

You may wish to back up your argument by the use of statistics – it is a ploy used by politicians, reporters and persuaders of all types. This is a valid use of evidence, but only if you have found the statistics in a reputable source and checked them at least once in other places.

As an example, look at this headline and subheading from October 2013:

AN ARMY OF DRUNK 11-YEAR-OLDS SWAMPING A&E DEPARTMENTS

Nearly 300 children aged 11 and under were admitted to A&E departments in the last year in alcohol-related incidents

On the face of it, 300 is a shocking statistic, but, is this really such a big number? There are 365 days in the year. So less than once a day, throughout the whole of the UK's hospitals, one child was admitted as 'alcohol related'. There are 700,000 11-year-olds, so the percentage of such children admitted is only 0.04 per cent. And 'alcohol-related' could mean not 'drunk', but a stone-cold sober child injured by someone who was drunk.

This headline is at least based on some actual figures, but there are far less reputable organisations (and reporters and politicians) who distort numbers past any point of truthfulness. For this reason it is your job, as a researcher, to check statistics against other sources. If the whole of your argument is based on a false statistic, which you have found but not checked, your essay will carry little weight.

As you were gathering your material you may have strengthened your original point of view, or moderated it a bit because of information that does not fit with your original thesis, or you might even have 'changed sides'.

Once you have decided what your point of view is, you now need to transmit it to your reader.

Organisation

Look at your notes/headings/extracts/statistics/evidence. You have probably gathered more material than you are going to be able to use. But that can be a good thing for two reasons.

1 You will be able to select the strongest points to promote your idea and fulfil your purpose.

2 You have a confidence-boosting command of your subject, which will allow you to change, rearrange or expand a point later on.

How you make a survey of your material is entirely up to you. It depends partly on whether you are basically a 'spatial' person or a 'list' person. Some people see connections in a spider diagram, and some in lists or tables.

Whichever of these you choose, you then have to select and arrange the points in a sensible order. Some of these are described below.

In an argumentative essay you would normally take at least two viewpoints into consideration and provide some evidence for each. But this does not mean that your own personal preference or point of view has to be suppressed. You can be fair, but you can also be very firm in your conclusion so long as it can be justified from the evidence you have presented.

In its simplest form you can deal with some points 'for' an idea/theory/ campaign and some points 'against'. Then you reach a conclusion that gives your own point of view, arising from the evidence you have presented.

This form has the advantage of clarity, but perhaps becomes rather 'listy' – **adding** ideas together rather than **developing** them.

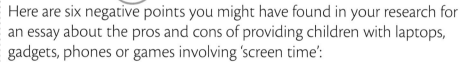

Exercise

Here are six negative points you might have found in your research for an essay about the pros and cons of providing children with laptops, gadgets, phones or games involving 'screen time':

1 expense
2 physical inactivity
3 lack of socialisation
4 isolation from family
5 stranger danger
6 creation of attention deficit.

You could simply write a paragraph about each of these items, then follow that with a number of advantages that you have found, and thus reach a conclusion based on the strength of each 'side'. This becomes simply a matter of addition, not of development.

Alternative approaches would be to:

● start with the less important items, building up to the most important (A)
● start with the really important, eye-catching item, then provide more evidence, again perhaps building up from the trivial to the more important ideas (B).

Try to arrange the six items above in order to achieve development A.

Then do the same for development B.

Another possible pattern is where each paragraph or section of the essay contains opposing points on one aspect of the topic. This keeps a balance in the argument, and can make things clearer to the reader.

Hints & tips

*Your choice of organisation depends on your material and what it is that **you** want to say to your reader. The important thing is that you have to think about your organisation, and try out various methods until you find the most satisfactory in terms of impact, interest and clarity.*

Linking

The linking of your ideas is, of course, an important aid to the development of your essay. There are numerous 'signpost' words that are useful both in your writing folio and in your critical essay work:

- **numeric:** *firstly, secondly, and finally*
- **contrasts:** *but, on the contrary, on the other hand, conversely*
- **intensifiers:** *and even more so, moreover, furthermore, without doubt*
- **causality:** *because of this, therefore, as a result*
- **time:** *once, in the past, nowadays, later, in the future.*

All of these are useful, but they should not be used slavishly or monotonously. You would be unlikely to use 'fifthly' or 'sixthly', for example. And there should certainly be strict rationing of 'furthermore' and 'moreover', which are often used mechanically and so lose their meaning or impact.

Often a more natural linkage is not dependent on single words or phrases, but in the continuation of thought from one paragraph to the next – you will come across many examples of this in your study of non-fiction texts for analysis (see pages 42–45).

For example, in an article about buying children gadgets as Christmas presents the link is made by the repetition of the idea of 'technology':

> . . . *Sociologists suggest that our increasing use of* **technology** *is making us more distracted and less able to be intimate with those around us.*

> **This technologising** *of Christmas, and our lives, can be* **charted** *through the list of the most popular gifts over the years . . .*

Try out various links. Don't be satisfied with the first one that comes to mind. There might be a more forceful (or a more subtle) way of doing it.

Use of illustration

Presenting a human interest example to engage the reader's emotions is another familiar device. For more on this see pages 46–47.

Persuasive essay

Many of the above steps are also necessary if you attempt the next suggested form of discursive essay – the persuasive essay. For example, linking words and the use of statistics are common to both types of writing.

This is probably best attempted if you have really strong feelings on your topic, and are convinced that your ideas are the right ones – even in the face of opposing evidence. Most teenagers perhaps would recognise this position!

Hints & tips

Before you hand in your final version, look at the advice under 'Editing' on pages 24–27.

Research

You still need to do some research – partly to find more evidence for your standpoint, but also to uncover any really obvious errors you might fall into. If you make an unwarranted statement such as 'All unemployed people are benefit scroungers', you will not shock the reader into taking your views seriously; you might put her or him off continuing to read your essay! Your evidence should be 'reliable'.

Organisation

See the advice given on page 5 on how to deal with your research.

When you have completed the survey of your research, you then have to select and arrange your points in a sensible and effective order to achieve your purpose – **persuasion**. The successful organisation of a persuasive essay is just as varied as that of an argumentative essay – and it depends on which audience you are trying to persuade.

Three possible patterns are:
1   Stick only to the evidence that supports your view, suppressing everything else. If you do this sufficiently intensely and forcefully, your reader may be carried along by your language and not stop to think of any contrary points.
2   Provide, in the course of your essay, a few counter arguments and then immediately demolish them. This can give the appearance of having taken everything into account, and therefore might make your essay more convincing.
3   Start out with seeming to accept the opposing view, lulling your reader into a (false) sense of security, before you gradually pile on the hammer blows for your own argument.

There are, of course, many other ways of approaching your material. You should experiment with different ordering, different climaxes until you find the one with most impact.

Linking

Linking is important in a persuasive essay, and all the suggestions on page 6 are useful. Added to those are such words as '**essentially**', '**effectively**', '**clearly**', '**basically**', '**obviously**', '**naturally**'. These words placed at the beginning of a sentence are designed to assume that the reader will agree with what follows. Of course, these words are used effectively in argumentative writing as well.

Rhetorical devices

There is a class of techniques that are especially useful in this context of persuasion (they are also used in argumentative writing). They are often called 'rhetorical devices' and include the following:
●   You are probably familiar with the idea of the rhetorical question. This is used to suggest that the answer to the question is self-evident; it is the writer's answer, and the reader is expected to agree with it.

- The climaxing of items in groups of three is often used as it seems to appeal to some deep language structures that we all recognise. Here is an example from an article entitled 'Have Foodies had their Day?':

    The fact remains, however, that despite the growth of farmers' markets, despite Jamie Oliver's ardent crusading, despite Michelle Obama's organic vegetable patch, gastroculture has done markedly little to improve the eating and cooking habits of most.

- The use of climax to strengthen or exaggerate an idea.
- The use of anti-climax to puncture an 'oppositional' idea.
- Repetition of all kinds, including a 'choral' start or finish to several paragraphs (as heard in Martin Luther King's 'I have a dream' speech). The danger with this is that such a device, unless used skilfully, can become mechanical and/or boring and predictable.

Use of illustration

Presenting a human interest example to engage the reader's emotions is another familiar device (see pages 46–47).

Use of statistics

See the advice on use of statistics in Argumentative essays (page 4).

Report

This form of writing, more perhaps than the previous two kinds, depends on how exactly the purpose of the report is matched to the expected reader. At Higher level, success is more likely if the purpose and audience are carefully defined, remembering always that the writing has to demonstrate the ability to encompass complexity and detail. There should be clear conclusions drawn from detailed evidence, taking into account, where necessary, possible alternatives. The language in which the report is written is likely to be precise but is less likely to demonstrate a wide spectrum of language devices. Extra material in the form of statistics, graphs, and so on, if well explained and integrated, can be included, but the writing is the most important part, and no additional marks are available for visual material.

Informative

This form of writing could be thought, at first, to be rather dull and mundane – simply producing facts. One of the main purposes of writing is to inform an audience of certain, usually important, material without a personal bias. Because you are writing a Higher essay, you have to remind yourself of the need for the subject to be of a complex nature. Try to achieve the level suggested by some of the bullet points in the list on page 2 – especially 'thematic concerns which are skilfully introduced and developed'.

> ### Hints & tips ★
>
> *A good test of the impact of your persuasive essay is to read it out loud to someone else, or even to yourself in the mirror. Are you convinced? If you are not, it is likely that others won't be either – so it is a good test to see if you need to go back to the draft and make some amends.*

The following example is an informative piece about *Voyager 1*, a space probe that started its voyage in 1977 (when the on-board computers were not even as sophisticated as an old-fashioned 'brick' phone). There are two versions of the piece. Version **A** informs us of the bare facts of the success of *Voyager* and is an edited version of **B**. Version **B** is the full text, written by Kevin Fong, co-director of the Centre for Altitude, Space and Extreme Environment Medicine. It informs us of the same facts but in an altogether more engaging way. It aims to make us interested in and excited by the information and thus more likely to remember it. Although each of these pieces is far too short to represent a folio piece, version **B** shows the kind of skills involved in good informative writing.

A: *Voyager 1* **continues its journey**	B: *Voyager 1* **keeps on trucking**
In November, a team of engineers at NASA's Jet Propulsion Laboratory signalled the old *Voyager 1* space probe, asking it to fire a set of thrusters that haven't been used for 37 years. It is more than 13 billion miles away now and has been exploring since its launch in 1977. No object made by humankind has ever journeyed so far; signals take over 19 hours travelling at the speed of light to reach it.	In November, a team of engineers at NASA's Jet Propulsion Laboratory signalled the ancient *Voyager 1* space probe, asking it to fire a set of thrusters that haven't been activated for 37 years. It is more than 13 billion miles away now and has been exploring since its launch in 1977. No object made by humankind has ever journeyed so far; signals take over 19 hours travelling at the speed of light to reach it.
Nevertheless it responded to the command, puffing hydrazine in short bursts, slowly rotating and successfully realigning its antenna, allowing it to be audible across space for a few more years to come. That movement became my favourite science moment of the year.	Nevertheless *Voyager* dutifully complied with the command, puffing hydrazine in precise millisecond bursts, gently rotating and successfully realigning its antenna, allowing it to be audible across the void for a few more years to come. That pirouette became my favourite science moment of the year.
Voyager 1 is out there in the darkness, moving in frictionless space, so distant from Earth now that it is nearly meaningless to describe the extent in any conventional unit of measurement. It has left behind the indefinite limit of our solar system and begun its long journey into interstellar space, but continues to gather and transmit information about the alien environment that surrounds it.	*Voyager 1* is out there in the darkness, coasting in the frictionless ocean of space, so distant from Earth now that it is nearly meaningless to describe the span in any conventional unit of measurement. It has left behind the indefinite edge of our solar system and begun its long journey into interstellar space, but continues to gather and transmit information about the alien environment that surrounds it.
That engineers can still find ways after all this time and space to make *Voyager* turn, allowing that huge triumph of science, engineering, technology and mathematics to keep in contact with us just a little longer is, I think, something worth celebrating.	That after all this time, and across all that space, engineers can still find ways to make *Voyager* do cartwheels, allowing that huge triumph of science, engineering, technology and mathematics to share its odyssey with us just a little longer is, I think, something worth celebrating.

Exercise

Make a note of what the differences are between version **A** and version **B**. Mostly it's just an added phrase, or a slightly different way of saying things. If there are two words that mean the same, such as 'used' and 'activated' in line 3 of each of the articles, think of why Kevin Fong has made his choice.

Next, look at the list of the differences you have found in version **B**. What comment could you make on Fong's word choice, imagery, or sentence structure? The skills you develop in the section on Understanding, Analysis and Evaluation are exactly the same skills you need to apply to your own writing to see whether or not it has 'impact'. Again, all skills in English are transferable: nothing is wasted.

Creative essays
Personal/reflective essay

On the face of it, this may seem an easier option than writing an imaginative piece. After all, you don't have to dream up ideas – you know who is involved and you know the circumstances because it is about you, and your reflection on that experience.

One of the problems with personal writing is that there are two purposes that are easily confused:

- **Writing as therapy**, where an attempt to record an experience is good for the emotional health of the writer.
- **Writing as art**, where the recording of an experience creates interest, sympathy, surprise and understanding in the reader (remember, the general heading for this type of essay is 'creative').

Occasionally, the first type (therapy) does meet the criteria for 'art'. It has to say something of more than merely personal significance. That is, it has to say something important to readers which has the potential to expand their understanding of some aspect of 'life, the universe and everything'.

Often, the therapy type of writing simply describes an important and sad event in the person's life, told in great detail, with an added-on reflective paragraph about the lessons learned from the experience.

Here's an example of this kind of tacked-on ending:

> I get upset every time I think about him not being there. One thing he taught me is never to take life for granted because you never know how long you have. If it wasn't for my grandad fighting his battle against illness and putting a smile on his face every day, I wouldn't be the person I am today. He taught me that no matter how bad things seem, enjoy life while you have it.

When well-handled, however, this kind of essay can succeed at Higher. That said, contrast this ending with the one on page 12, which is a more thoughtful and measured conclusion to the essay.

This does not mean that writing as therapy is of no value. It is one of the gifts that literacy gives us. We can attempt to come to terms with the agony and the ecstasy of our own lives through writing accounts, poetry and song, and it is good for us. But perhaps it is not so meaningful for a wider audience. So maybe it would be wise to consider carefully before presenting it as your best creative piece.

Writing a personal/reflective essay that is 'creative' demands some of the elements of shaping and structuring that you would use in a short story. The reflective element is best demonstrated throughout the essay, not necessarily by **saying** that you learned something, but more by **showing** that you grew throughout the experience as a person in understanding of, or 'insight' into, your own growth and development.

Many submissions are related to death or divorce. These are difficult situations, and cause profound feelings of loss and despair, but to transmit those feelings effectively to a reader is quite difficult.

> *Hints & tips*
>
> The personal essay at Higher level should show a degree of reflection and give a sense of the writer's personality.

Suppose you have been writing about the death of your grandmother, and at some point you say 'I miss her so much'. How is that 'missing' felt? In the emptiness of a room? In a message that never comes? In a missing place at the table? These are details that make much clearer, and more poignant, the actual 'missingness' and may cause the reader to empathise with your experience.

Another common topic is an event from early childhood. The event has remained in the memory, but the element of hindsight and distance takes the edge off the sharpness of the experience. A 6-year-old does not think or see things in the same way a 16-year-old does.

Suppose that, in the course of such an essay, you remember (aged 6):

> *My father started to cry. I had never seen him cry before. It was heartbreaking.*

Without careful and precise use of language, your memory, or your language (or both!) risk not carrying a feeling of authenticity to your reader: to avoid this, you could add something to show you are commenting from the perspective of being 16:

> *My father started to cry. I had never seen him cry before. Looking back, I remember it as being heartbreaking.*

Remember

There is a whole list of common phrases which, while true, are not particular and individualised enough to convey to an outsider (your reader) a feeling of empathy or sympathy — they become a little like a cliché. Here are a few such phrases:

☞ *He was my best friend ever.*
☞ *I was being torn in two.*
☞ *She was always there for me.*
☞ *He always understood.*

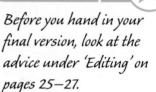

Hints & tips

Before you hand in your final version, look at the advice under 'Editing' on pages 25–27.

There can, however, be very powerful writing in this genre in the hands of a writer who is willing to work, shape and craft the experience – sad or happy – into a piece of 'creative' writing.

You could also write about your experience of a particular pastime, or idea, or cause, or thought as it has happened in your life. It could be:

- a reflection dealt with in a concerned or contemplative tone – an insight into an aspect of society, adding to your understanding and self-knowledge arising from your own experience

or

- a reflection on aspects of life and your place within it dealt with ironically, whimsically or humorously, such as:
  - an essay on possessions/fashion and how important they are to your self-image
  - an essay on the trauma caused by separation from your life support system – your mobile phone.

There is a possibility that this kind of essay can veer into the discursive, but the element of personal experience keeps it firmly within the reflective zone.

Example 1

Here is the opening of an essay entitled 'Am I a Patriot?'

> *My grandfather was a patriot: all his generation, it seems, were and are. He was fluent in several languages and loved to travel – but although he never belittled other countries, his was the greatest nation on earth. It was the place he felt at home, the only place that really did everything right.*
>
> *My grandmother, too, on the other side – she was a patriot. She would mutter under her breath about 'that Gobbles and Hitler'. Woe to anyone who, playing with model battleships, let the Bismarck win. She travelled too – though never to Germany – but she always yearned for home. Her own house, the talk of her own people, these were the things that mattered.*
>
> *Both, I am sure, wanted me to love my country – their country.*
>
> *But my grandfather considered himself 'English through and through'. For him, this meant admiring the Empire – he believed that the British were somehow better at many things than those over whom they once ruled. For her part, my grandmother regarded herself as one of those people who my grandfather's race had ruled – or oppressed – for she was, 'through and through', a Scot, from the island of Lewis.*

The body of the essay goes on to look at the different characteristics of the English and the Scots as experienced through his grandparents, and comes to a conclusion:

> *I do not resent English people. I cannot – I loved my grandfather, and much of my blood is their blood.*
>
> *Individually, of course – the English are people like any others. But can I love my grandfather's concept of that nation?*
>
> *That vision, that patriotic sense of nationhood, that I cannot share. I might respect the English for their historical achievements but at the same time, to my grandmother, they were the people who viewed my Scottish ancestors merely as remote highlanders.*
>
> *But I cannot love my grandmother's version of Scotland either. My grandmother's views were hidebound, narrow and limited. Her concerns were often petty – and her moaning was never-ending.*
>
> . . .
>
> *I have seen the homes of my ancestors from both sides of the barriers. I cannot hate what I have seen, but I cannot choose a side because I have seen both sides through the eyes of the other. I can never reject those places my grandparents loved. For me, being a patriot would mean accepting one fully, and having to reject the other, and this is impossible for me. So, in the end, I answer the initial question of the title of this essay. I cannot choose and so I cannot be a patriot.*

Because the viewpoint throughout is based firmly in the writer's own and his family's experience and emotions, this is an effective reflective essay. It could cause the reader to reflect on her or his own definition and views of patriotism, and so it is effective in achieving its purpose.

It also demonstrates the qualities of characterisation (you can 'see' his grandfather and grandmother) and has structural strengths in the way the end recalls the beginning and the title.

This kind of reflective essay would be acceptable if you are thinking of putting together a Creative Writing Folio as part of the Advanced Higher English course next year.

Example 2

You could imagine a similar essay dealing with your relationship with your smartphone.

Opening:

> *I will switch off my phone every evening. I will. I'm not going to be a slave like everyone else.*

> *I will hide it.*

> *I will lock it in a cupboard and throw away the key.*

This sets the scene for a discussion/reflection on the issue.

The body of the essay would now be about your struggles with the deprivation, your thoughts about your own strengths and weaknesses, your alienation from your friends … the advantages of having more time to do other more creative things, rediscovering the pleasures of reading/hobbies/homework(?).

Conclusion (possibly):

> *Lying in the dark, its calm blue glow bathing the scene, my indispensable friend.*

Hints & tips ⭐

Before you hand in your final version, look at the advice under 'Editing' on pages 25—27.

As a reader you know which side has won, and you know something about the self-knowledge (or lack of it) of the writer. It has said something interesting to readers (the potential audience), which has the purpose of making them look at the topic with a fresh insight.

Imaginative piece

This essay can be in any genre you have practised and feel comfortable with. The most common forms are considered in this section.

Short story

This is one of the genres of imaginative writing that you have probably been writing since you were in primary school. Looking at this genre as practised by professional writers can help to inform your own writing.

The techniques of prose fiction are covered in Chapter 5 in the section on Critical Essays (page 133). The most important devices to consider are **plot**, **structure**, **characterisation** and **setting**. Ideally, you should be able to look at your own work in the same way that you have looked at the work of professional writers.

Plot

The hardest aspect of short stories is plotting. There are often many good and promising openings, lots of subtle characterisation, atmospheric settings, great tension or suspense. But quite often this all leads to a predictable, banal or impossible ending – a suicidal dive off the high building, which is roughly equivalent to the primary school ending: 'I woke up and it was all a dream!'

Here is an example of this kind of artificially 'surprising' ending to a short story called 'The Scream':

> *I passed through the chipped and peeling gates to my new school. A newspaper blew into my side. I read the headline. It read 'RIP to Jade Wilson who died age 15 on the 13th of March 2003'. That's me, I thought, but then what made it worse was the date of the paper, 13th of March 2003. My name is Jade Wilson. I died ten years ago.*

Effective plots have to do more than carry the story – they should allow the theme(s) of the short story to emerge. How will the reader's understanding of the human condition be enlarged by your story? Will your reader's sympathies be engaged by your character(s) and their fate(s)? Will reading leave your reader content/shocked/amused/sad/apprehensive?

Suppose, for example, that you have decided to write in the science fiction genre. Perhaps the plot concerns some cataclysmic event threatening the human race caused by our misuse of the environment. Is your writing powerful enough to create sympathy for the protagonist(s), or to generate anger directed at the 'misusers'?

Remember

There should be nothing in your story that does not contribute to the final purpose of the story. Anything that you mention as part of the setting or details of the incident should be there for a reason. If you note on the mantelpiece of the room a large brass ornament, that ornament has to be used, or deliberately not used. It cannot – in a classic narrative structure – be ignored once it has been mentioned.

Methods of narration

There are various methods of narration that you can use. The most common are:

1 first-person narrator
2 third-person narrator – omniscient or restricted
3 a split narrative
4 a framed narrative
5 a reliable or unreliable narrator.

Methods 1 and 2 are quite straightforward. Methods 3, 4 and 5 are a bit more complex and need careful handling.

These methods are illustrated using the following scenario.

> A large untidy man enters an office to start a new job. His boss is a woman who has employed him against her better judgement. She seems to have been leaned on by someone to take the man on. The man's experience in this job (possibly pressure from the woman) causes him to have some sort of extreme reaction, and results in a subsequent, unexpected incident.

Method 1: First-person narrative appears to be an easy option, as you can let the reader know the inmost thoughts of your main character. But it has limitations.

● It can become monotonous – I did, I felt, I saw.
● It is more difficult to paint a clear idea of the thoughts of others (although dialogue may help).
● It does not allow for action at which the 'I' is not present.

Using our office scenario:

> *I walked into the room for only the second time. The interview had been different. This was the real thing. A mixture of anticipation, anxiety and curiosity filled my thoughts as I walked towards my new boss, hand held out in greeting. She ignored it, scanned me from top to toe, frowned and left the room.*

The story may then go on to catalogue the trials and tribulations of the protagonist in his first day in a new job, but because it is a first-person narrative, we don't have any means of knowing what the boss actually thinks. There are ways round that:

- dialogue where the boss says what the problem is
- an incident from which the reader can infer the boss's thoughts
- a device, such as a note left on a table or an email on a screen.

So, you have to be aware that there are problems to solve.

Method 2: Third-person narrative is the most common narrative method for fiction. An omniscient narrator can tell you what everyone is thinking and provide a straightforward reading.

> *He walked into the room for only the second time. The interview had been different. This was the real thing. A mixture of anticipation, anxiety and curiosity filled his thoughts as he walked towards his new boss, hand held out in greeting. She ignored it, scanned him from top to toe, frowned and left the room, asking herself if she had done the right thing in hiring such an untidy, shambolic specimen. She had been leant on heavily to give him the job but perhaps she should have resisted the pressure.*

Here, you can see both sides of the incident, but perhaps the omniscient narrator has let us see too much, too soon.

Method 3: A **split narrative** can help to achieve a compromise between first- and third-person narratives, but it is quite difficult to handle and can hold up the pace of the narrative.

> *I walked into the room for only the second time. The interview had been different. This was the real thing. A mixture of anticipation, anxiety and curiosity filled my thoughts as I walked towards my new boss, hand held out in greeting. She ignored it, scanned me from top to toe, frowned and left the room.*
>
> *What can I have been thinking of? He looked mildly untidy at the interview, but this – he doesn't even look clean. It's one thing to do a favour for an old friend's son – OK, more than a favour, a necessary recompense, a gun to my head – but . . .*

The problem is how you sustain a narrative like this without it becoming too bitty, and eventually monotonous. The key, of course, is to keep the momentum of the story going, not just cutting it up arbitrarily into chunks. Your two narrators have to carry a convincing plot line so use contrast, parallels, or reversals to keep the characters interesting.

> ### Hints & tips ★
>
> *A restricted third-person narrative is one where all the events in the book are seen from the point of view of the main character. An example of this kind of writing is Ernest Hemingway's* For Whom the Bell Tolls *in which the main character Robert Jordan carries almost all of the actions and thoughts in the novel. The restricted third-person narrative has the same difficulties as a first-person narrative – you can only know what he or she knows/sees/hears personally.*

Method 4: A **framed narrative**, or a narrative using a framing device, can also be effective. It allows you to make the reader look more objectively at the main character. It often reveals the fate of the character right at the beginning of the story, so that you focus on the process of how he/she got there.

In this example, the speaker in the framing device is a psychiatrist who is treating the main character in our office scenario after his breakdown.

> *My first sight of him was when he slid silently into my consulting room as if on a breath of insubstantial wind. Over the next weeks and months I never did have a solid grip on his ethereal presence or on his equally ethereal mind. His story slipped and changed shape as we talked, but I had the impression of some utter truth – hidden from both of us. When I pieced it together much later it began to make a kind of crazy sense. What follows is as near as I can get to a coherent pattern and chronology.*

What follows might be the story of the big shambolic guy and how through some strange conflict with his employer he has been stripped of his physique, personality, sanity even – and perhaps what form his terrible retribution took, leading to the 'consultations'. The end paragraph returns to the psychiatrist.

> *As I say, I tended to believe him, in the face of all the evidence. In the twists of his labyrinthine mind, he was right, and he was justified. His very quietude convinced me personally. But to my everlasting shame, in my professional capacity, I had to throw him to the wolves. And I did.*

Method 5: A **reliable or unreliable narrator** – the general assumption is that the narrator – first, third, split or framer – is going to be reliable. If the narrator is going to prove to be unreliable, the writer should give the reader some hint to follow, and even if the revelation of the unreliability comes at the end it must be credible. It is not a 'Get out of jail free' card.

Structure

A sound structure can help your plotting to achieve an effective shape.

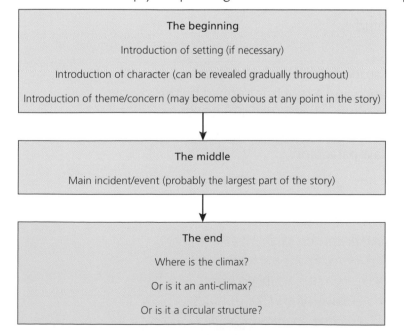

The beginning

Introduction of setting (if necessary)

Introduction of character (can be revealed gradually throughout)

Introduction of theme/concern (may become obvious at any point in the story)

The middle

Main incident/event (probably the largest part of the story)

The end

Where is the climax?

Or is it an anti-climax?

Or is it a circular structure?

Hints & tips ★

Paragraphing is just as important here as it is in discursive essays. You may not have 'topic sentences' in the sense that you need them in discursive writing but each paragraph has a part to play in providing stepping stones for understanding a character, for moving the plot on or for providing a contrast important in a conflict.

Characterisation

In a short story, which usually concerns itself with one defined incident, you don't usually need a large cast of characters. As one of the basic elements of short-story narrative is conflict, you generally need at least two but, of course, the main character can be in conflict with himself or with his environment rather than with another human being.

What the character does, says and thinks, and what is said about or thought about her or him are the usual elements of characterisation, but not necessarily all of these, and we often don't need to know physical characteristics unless they are going to be important in the narrative.

> *She was blonde, about 30, with dark blue eyes.*

Probably this description is unnecessary, as it is just a standard description of a young woman, whose looks may, or may not, be important for the plot.

> *A face too long, eyes too wide, too pale. First impressions are sometimes wrong – and sometimes not.*

If that description were to be used, it would be **because** there is some sort of excess suggested – perhaps a character who overdramatises or goes too far.

Setting in place/setting in time

As with the physical descriptions of characters, the first question you need to ask yourself about setting is: do we need to know? If the answer is 'yes', then the second question is: how much do we need to know? Consider the following:

- If your scenario is an office, it is likely that this will become obvious from the activities described, without the setting having to be described explicitly.
- If, on the other hand, your story is set in the past, or the future, your reader might find it helpful to be given that information sooner rather than later.
- If you choose to start your story with an evocative description of a place, there has to be a purpose behind it.

Example

In the following example from a short story called 'Drifting', the first paragraph, with its description of a branch and a beach, is justified by the following paragraph in which the characters appear in the setting. When you reach the end of the story, it is obvious that the first paragraph is setting up the symbolic nature of the last paragraph.

> *The ancient and smoothed branch bobs gently in the push and pull of an oncoming tide. Its surface is bleached and featureless, long since removed of all the blemishes that once identified it, and now it floats alone on a vast grey featureless plain. With no direction of its own, and no vitality in its dead core, the branch is swept towards a beach by strong currents that it no longer has the strength to fight. It moves yet more slowly now in the shallows of the small bay. It is here that it will rest, after the next high tide.*

The branch nudges lightly against a leg. The leg stands upright in the water, unflinching despite the cold. The skin on it looks delicate, like an old sheet of parchment, a memorial of lives long in the past; it is as much lacking in vitality as the log. Further up this leg is the hemline of a faded summer dress, the colours shadows of ancient buds. The dress hangs limp against a frame that in days gone by was full. Her face was once radiant, her lips deep, and her hair an intense copper. Now everything is grey and withered, her lips blue.

The boy standing and watching the woman from a distance is me.

The central part of the story gradually reveals the dementia of the grandmother and the effect of this on the boy who loves her and cannot bear to see her suffer.

The concentration of pain that I see all around her, the remains of humanity long past its span, drive me to crave her freedom.

I feel an overwhelming urge to give these shadows an end, to allow them to escape into nothingness.

My grandmother turns to me. In her eyes there is light but also fear. She doesn't know where she is or who I am. I smile. Bidding her follow me, I take her by the arm and lead her through the dunes and back up towards the path, and the cliff – and the edge.

Night comes with a storm. Rain beats down on the ground, washing the sand and the dunes and the cliff. The wind has changed. The water becomes rough and the log is thrown by wave after wave. The churning water grows higher, the wind faster, never subsiding. The log is cast high in the air, its end spears deep into the beach and it is buried by wave upon wave and then sand.

In the pale and pink light of dawn the still-wet sand is smooth. The log is gone. In the sand it rests protected and out of reach; no longer bothered by the cruelty of the wind or the sea. It has achieved peace.

The forms of short stories we have looked at in the last seven pages are probably those most familiar to you. There are, however, many other forms – post-modern forms, magical realism, stream of consciousness – which you can attempt if you have discussed and practised them. You can also try other forms of prose fiction – a chapter from a novel, for example – but you must always be aware of the conventions of the genre you have chosen.

Poetry

There is no reason why you shouldn't try to write in this genre. It is the most concentrated expression of ideas and emotion, but it is a craft you have to practise. Not all poems that you write will be good enough to present as an item in your folio, but the more you practise the more opportunity you will have to create and develop poems that work.

Some pieces of poetry written for the folio resemble prose chopped up into lines (as in the case of Example 1 below). This can work, when handled skilfully, with close attention to how the piece sounds. If the line breaks pay due attention to both the sense and the rhythm of the language, it is possible to regard the result as an example of free verse. In comparing the next two examples, you should be able to see the difference between the two poems.

The best test is to read both out loud. The reading should show you the natural flow of thought in the second example, as opposed to some of the rather arbitrary breaks in the first.

Example 1

Night comes with a storm.
Rain beats down on the ground
washing the sand and the dunes and the cliff.*
The wind has changed.
5   The water becomes rough
and the log is thrown by wave after wave.*
The churning water grows higher,
the wind faster, never subsiding.
The log is cast high in the air –
10 its end spears deep into the beach
and it is buried by wave upon wave and then sand.*
In the pale and pink light of dawn
the still-wet sand is smooth.
The log is gone.
15 In the sand it rests protected and out of reach;*
no longer bothered by the cruelty of the wind or the sea.*
It has achieved peace.

The first extract you will recognise as the same words used in the end of the short story 'Drifting' on pages 18–19. Although full of description, it has several long lines marked with an asterisk (*) which are difficult to say, and there does not really seem to be a reason for their length.

In contrast, when reading the example below out loud, you will realise that Ferlinghetti's lines force you into getting the sense of the movement of the eye over Klimt's painting.

Example 2

The Kiss – Short Story on a Painting of Gustav Klimt (extract lines 1–25)

They are kneeling upright on a flowered bed

He

     has just caught her there

        and holds her still

5   Her gown

     has slipped down

        off her shoulder

He has an urgent hunger

    His dark head

10   bends to hers

      hungrily

And the woman the woman

   turns her tangerine lips from his

   one hand like the head of a dead swan

15   draped down over

      his heavy neck

   the fingers

    strangely crimped

    tightly together

20 her other arm doubled up

    against her tight breast

    her hand a languid claw

      clutching his hand

   which would turn her mouth

25   to his

Lawrence Ferlinghetti

The other difference of course, is that the Ferlinghetti poem is describing something about a physical relationship, which, in very deft and swift lines, sketches in the characterisation of the man and the woman. The reader becomes an observer of the action. The other poem about the log is not really doing anything except giving a description. On its own it has very little to say to the reader.

Poetry in a particular form

You may choose to write in a particular form, such as a sonnet, a ballad or in rhyming couplets, but the problem in the less successful attempts is that the rhyme and form become the weights that hold the poem down with twisted phrases and unlikely words. Look at the examples below.

Example 1

Hoping always to see your eyes track me down

Through the long reaches of the coming day

I find instead my eyes on you do frown

Waiting for the response from you to come my way.

5 Why do I always have to make the first move

Your avoiding me seems to me so cruel.

What do I have to do to prove

My love for you needs no more fuel.

It will burn for you eternally in a flame

10 Fed always by the passion of my heart.

Even in the face of your indifference

My love for you will stay the same,

As right from the beginning, right from the start,

Although I know you only keep me on sufferance.

Example 2

Suburban Sonnet

She practises a fugue, though it can matter

to no one now if she plays it well or not.

Beside her on the floor two children chatter,

then scream and fight. She hushes them. A pot

5 boils over. As she rushes to the stove

too late, a wave of nausea overpowers

subject and counter-subject. Zest and love

drain out with soapy water as she scours

the crusted milk. Her veins ache. Once she played

10 for Rubenstein*, who yawned. The children caper

round a sprung mousetrap, where a mouse lies dead.

When the soft corpse won't move they seem afraid.

She comforts them; and wraps it in a paper

featuring: *Tasty dishes from stale bread.*

Gwen Harwood

* Rubenstein was a famous pianist and composer.

If you compare these two poems, both in sonnet form, you can see that the second is much more original.

In the first example, the word order seems more forced, to accommodate the rhyme in lines 3 and 6, the problem of trying to find a rhyme for 'indifference' in line 11, and several lines that are too long to say with any ease.

Overall, this poem does not say as much as the other. Almost every line is a cliché:

'My love for you needs no more fuel';

'eternally in a flame';

'the passion of my heart'.

As everything is rather generalised, there is no sense of a particular idea or person. The reader, in this case, has not really learned anything specific, so the poem has not been as successful as it could have been.

In contrast, the second sonnet flows naturally, with the rhyme acting subtly as a substructure to give form to the poem, but it is also saying to the reader something quite profound about lost hopes, the trap that closes on 'the housewife' persona. Notice how no words are wasted. The trapped mouse is important, and so is the headline featured in the last line. The reader's understanding of the housewife and her predicament is expanded by the poem.

Drama script

There are several forms this genre can take.

Self-contained scene/sketch

Most of the advice about short stories also applies to this form. That is, the piece of writing has to say something important to the potential audience, something which has the purpose of expanding our understanding of some aspect of life or to make us look at something with new insight. Within this genre, plot, structure and characterisation have to do the same job as in a short story.

It is actually quite difficult to manage all this within the course of a dramatic script. You normally do not have a narrator. The story must unfold though the dialogue of the characters, which does not allow you to take shortcuts into letting the audience read their thoughts.

Remember

By all means try poetry, but beware of these three major pitfalls:

☞ Is it poetry, or is it just poetic prose?

☞ Is your attempt at form/rhyme imposing too much on the subject of your poem?

☞ Have you tried to avoid cliché or overly generalised language?

Read your poem out loud to help you detect these problems.

There are ways around this.

- You can have a narrator as a character.
- You can use soliloquies or asides to the audience.
- You can use stage/technical directions.

All of these, however, need to be handled with care – too many stage directions often mean that the dialogue is too weak to carry the line of thought/emotion. Soliloquies and asides can interfere with the 'naturalistic' feel of a piece, so consider carefully whether they fit with the genre you are aiming for. A narrator can be quite tricky to handle. She or he acts as an intermediary between actor and audience, but also distances the actors from the audience. This can prevent (sometimes deliberately) the audience's sympathies from being maintained.

Monologue

Monologue may appear to be an easier option, but, in fact, it isn't. A monologue is often just a first-person narrative delivering a not very effective story. So all the problems that arise in trying to write an effective first-person narrative in fiction also apply to monologues. The stage directions are the only technique that differentiate the monologue from the short story. While these directions can suggest events offstage, the plot, structure and characterisation still have to be skilful and creative.

> ### Hints & tips
>
> #### Advice for all dramatic scripts
>
> *Speak them out loud. Get friends to read them out loud. Do the words sound as if they are the words of real people? Would anyone actually say that? This is the final test you must apply to your work. If it fails this test then you have to rewrite it.*

Editing
Technical aspects

This process is almost as important as the writing was in the first place. When you have what you think is your final draft, there are several checks you must make:

- **Capitalisation** has to be consistent. Names of places and people are easy, but names of organisations and events are more difficult. If you are writing a political essay about Parliament, the Church, the State or the Law, you have to remain consistent. In sporting terms, the League Cup or a Grand Slam have to have their capital letters. It is just a matter of taking care. The most important function is, of course, at the beginning of sentences.
- **Spelling** has to be checked, either in dictionaries or by spellcheck – but remember that spellcheck can get it wrong if your initial spelling is too far from being correct. And it can't pick up on common errors such as *of/off*, *there/their*, *it's/its*, which can let you down so badly.

> ### Remember
>
> Your layout of such details as speakers/stage directions/technical specifications should be clear and in line with the conventional ways of dealing with a drama script.

> ### Hints & tips
>
> *Note the following SQA definition of technical accuracy to guide the examiners who mark your work:*
>
> *Few errors are present: paragraphs, sentences and punctuation are mostly accurate and organised so that the writing is clearly and readily understood; spelling errors (particularly of high frequency words) are infrequent.*
>
> *It is vital therefore that you check your work for errors and inconsistencies in **capitalisation, spelling** and **sentencing**.*

- **Sentencing** that is poor means your writing may not communicate meaning at first reading. There are many rules to help you to get your sentencing right. If you are unsure, one helpful test is to look at each sentence you have written – from the capitalised word at the beginning to the full stop at the end. Read it out loud in isolation from the rest of your essay. Does it make sense? Where you pause to take a breath is often an indication that there should be punctuation of some kind. Is there? Should it be a comma or a full stop? The answers to these questions will create more accuracy in your writing. It will take some time to treat each one of your sentences in this way, but it will be worth it. Note that in some essays and in some styles sentencing may not be standard, and this is perfectly acceptable if it is effective in creating an impact.
- **Proof reading** is essential. After all your editing and care, if you leave obvious typos, they will be counted as errors. You may say that your finger just hit the wrong key, or the paste command did not do what you wanted it to do. But all that is your problem. They are your errors, not the computer's.

Structure and organisation (especially in discursive essays)

Paragraphing is important in giving shape to your essay. For each paragraph you need to ask yourself:
- What is the topic?
- What are the points being made?
- How does the paragraph help to develop the overall argument?
- How does each paragraph link with the next in a logical way?

And for the whole essay ask yourself:
- How does the overall structure of the essay promote the conclusion?

In Chapter 2 Reading Skills you will find a more detailed discussion on the use of topic sentences (page 34); in Chapter 3 Reading for Understanding, Analysis and Evaluation you will find more guidance on how points are made (pages 39–41); how arguments are developed (pages 41–42) and in what ways links are effective (pages 42–45). See also the section about the effectiveness of a conclusion on pages 47–49.

Cutting out unnecessary detail

Consider a personal/reflective essay that begins:

> *I was so looking forward to this holiday. The morning we were leaving for the airport, my brother Tommy decided he was feeling sick, but he was bundled into the car anyway by my frustrated father and my harassed mother, along with my baby sister Eveline. We just got there in time to check in and then we were able to relax with a cup of coffee.*

This paragraph contains a lot of unnecessary detail, which is preventing the reader from getting to the heart of the experience. The first sentence

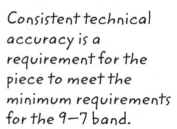
Remember

Consistent technical accuracy is a requirement for the piece to meet the minimum requirements for the 9–7 band.

"I was so looking forward to this holiday" is a good opening. It suggests to the reader that either the holiday presented the writer with some magical and transforming experience, or hints at the possibility that the holiday was a disaster. It would be better to skip the airport details and move straight onto the holiday itself.

Cutting out unnecessary words/phrases

Practice paragraph

> The two excited children came out of the busy café with sticky red raspberry ice lollies, juice making red tracks down their little hands. They stopped at the edge of the busy street watching for a space in the dense noisy traffic to cross safely to the other pavement crowded with bustling shoppers all dressed in summer dresses and bright T-shirts with slogans on. A kindly middle-aged woman, dressed in green, saw them standing there and came up to them and took their sticky little hands to help them over the noisy street. On the other side the two little children ran down the shaded narrow alley where they were to meet their mother.

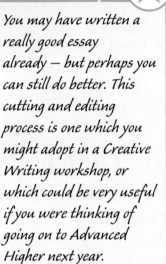

Hints & tips

You may have written a really good essay already — but perhaps you can still do better. This cutting and editing process is one which you might adopt in a Creative Writing workshop, or which could be very useful if you were thinking of going on to Advanced Higher next year.

Many of these descriptive words are unnecessary. See how many you can cut out. You should find at least 12.

On a more advanced level, skilled writers have to learn that sometimes they have to cut out words they like, and have worked hard to use, but which actually are redundant. The paragraph below is already of a good standard and would score well at Higher. However, there is no harm in looking at techniques for editing which could help it do even better after some editing. These techniques can be applied to all types of writing, at Higher and beyond.

Original first paragraph

> The ancient and smoothed branch bobs gently in the push and pull of an oncoming tide. Its surface is bleached and featureless, long since removed of all the blemishes that once identified it, and now it floats alone on a vast grey featureless plain. With no direction of its own, and no vitality in its dead core, the branch is swept towards a beach by strong currents that it no longer has the strength to fight. It moves yet more slowly now in the shallows of the small bay. It is here that it will rest, after the next high tide. (101 words)

'removed of' doesn't make a lot of sense, and does it matter that it once had 'blemishes'?

'vast' is not needed, as 'plain' on its own suggests a large expanse.

The tide is coming in, not out: 'pull' is confusing.

Repetition of 'featureless'. Is this clumsy, or does the repetition reinforce the idea? The answer could be either, but the question should be asked.

Editing process

The ancient and smoothed branch bobs gently in the push ~~and pull~~ of an oncoming tide. Its surface is bleached and ⟨featureless⟩, ~~long since removed of all the blemishes that once identified it, and now it floats~~ <u>floating</u> alone on a ~~vast~~ grey ⟨featureless⟩ plain. With no direction of its own, and no vitality in its dead core, ~~the branch is swept towards a beach by strong currents that it no longer has the strength to fight.~~ it moves yet more slowly ~~now~~ in the shallows of the small bay. It is here that it will rest, ~~after~~ <u>at</u> the next high tide.

Why does the branch move from 'bobbing gently' to 'swept . . . by strong currents' then back to 'moves yet more slowly'?

'after' suggests two tides, not one.

There has been no shift in time, we are still in the present.

Edited version

The ancient and smoothed branch bobs gently in the push of an oncoming tide. Its surface is bleached and featureless, floating alone on a grey featureless plain. With no direction of its own, and no vitality in its dead core, it moves yet more slowly in the shallows of the small bay. It is here that it will rest, at the next high tide. (64 words)

This is an even tighter piece of writing; through editing, the writer is consciously attempting to use language in a detailed and complex way, and to a large extent he succeeds. By editing your work to the best possible standard, you are offering the marker a text where the strengths are obvious in a holistic view of the whole piece. The advice and guidance in this chapter should help you to minimise your weaknesses and add to your strengths, leading to a reward in the form of high marks.

Remember

Your marker is always looking to mark positively. This means they will focus on the strengths of your writing, and only look at the weaknesses if they have a significant impact on the overall piece. People always make mistakes — but your piece does not need to be perfect to gain full marks.

Chapter 2

Reading skills

Not surprisingly the best preparation for approaching a reading exam is to read. But how much? How often? You have to practise reading as you have to practise any other skill.

There are, of course, questions that you have to learn how to answer, but unless you can practise reading a lot, and regularly, until you are comfortable with the kinds of texts you may be faced with, the questions will remain difficult.

The first necessary skill is to gain an **overview** of an article on a topic or an account of an event.

After that each **paragraph** will contain a step in the 'argument' of the piece.

Finally, each **sentence** will contain some detail necessary for a full understanding of the text.

Overview

You will make a more positive start on your first reading of a piece of prose if you know what it is about before you begin. Newspapers use headlines for this very purpose. They also use subheadings and highlighted extracts, all of which are meant to catch your eye and seduce you into reading further.

Example 1

THE TRUTH ABOUT LIFE AS A HOUSEHUSBAND
200,000 British men now stay home to look after the children

So what's it like being a man in a woman's world? **Jon Absalom**, *who gave up his career, tells all!*

These three items (the heading, subheading and introduction) all stand out typographically in the article so that before you read it, you know the subject will be about dads who stay at home, and the possible problems associated with such a lifestyle choice.

Your reading will now be an **informed** reading, giving focus to your thoughts.

Example 2

FATHERS SPURN PLAN TO SAVE PARENTS FROM COURT BATTLES

Government unveils scheme to encourage mediation in contact rows

In this case you know to expect some explanation of an attempt to get (separated) parents to agree about contact time with their children instead of going to court. You also know that some fathers don't think the plan will help them much. As a result you will be on the lookout for what the plan is and why the fathers are against it. Again, you start your reading with some knowledge of what is likely to appear. You are informed and focused.

Note: 'typographically', 'spurn' and 'mediation' are words used on page 28 and this page. If you don't know what they mean, look them up. And don't worry. The more you read, the more familiar you will become with 'high order' words.

Training for reading

You can train yourself into being a good reader, just as you can train for a sport or a craft. It may not initially be very pleasant, but if you stick with it you will make progress.

If you already read most of a quality daily paper or most of one of the Sunday 'heavies', and a couple of novels a month, with an occasional biography or historical/scientific text thrown in, not to mention two or three Shakespeare plays by way of bedtime reading, then you probably don't need to read the next section. But if that is several miles away from describing what you do, then you should keep right on reading.

 *Exercise*

You might wish to use the Approach to Reading form on page 31 to help you.

1 Find a newspaper or magazine article that attracts you because of the headline, the subject, a photograph or some interesting graphics.
2 Look at the headline, any subheadings, highlighted quotations, photo captions, etc.
3 Ask yourself: 'What do I expect to find out by reading this?'
4 Read the article.
5 Ask yourself: 'What have I found out?'
6 Write down the main ideas in note form.
7 Consider if there are any clues about the writer's stance on the topic.

Hints & tips

*The kind of articles you need will be found in newspapers such as the **Herald** or the **Scotsman**. Weekend editions, especially the **WEEKEND i** contain thoughtful articles reflecting on news stories. These are probably a better source than the original news story as there is more likely to be an 'argument' rather than simply an account of events. Other possibilities include **The Times**, the **Guardian**, the **Telegraph**, the **Independent** and their Sunday counterparts, including the **Observer**. Comment and lifestyle sections often offer good reading opportunities. There are also periodicals that cover special interest groups such as **New Scientist**, **The Economist**, **New Statesman** and the **Spectator**. Reputable sources on the internet can also provide you with similar reading experiences.*

Depending on the difficulty of the article you have chosen you might find that you have understood most of what is said, in which case you can answer the questions and move on.

If you are having difficulty, is your lack of understanding because:
a) you don't understand some of the vocabulary?
b) you get lost in the line of thought?

If a) is the problem, get down to work with a dictionary. If b) is the problem, read each paragraph individually, and see what meaning you can make of it.

When you have done that, give the article a final reading and see if you can make better notes (step 6 on page 29).

Repeat this exercise weekly till the exam. Even though you don't feel you are making progress, you will be. Like training for anything, doing a little often is more effective than a big blitz just before the competition.

Another way of approaching this exercise is to give the article to someone else to read after you have read it – anyone who has reading skills equal to or better than your own (long-suffering parents, friendly adults, charitable elder sisters or brothers) – and tell them what you think the main points are. You are having to put your thoughts into words, and if your 'sharer' comes up with other thoughts and ideas then this will add to your understanding of the piece.

If you find yourself understanding the articles 100 per cent at first reading, you need to move on to more difficult articles or to articles on subjects you know nothing about, so that you have to work harder. As in all training – no pain, no gain.

The Approach to Reading form on the next page may be a useful tool for you as you continue to work on your reading skills.

Approach to Reading

Training Programme for Close Reading

Preparation

Note down   Headline

```



```

Note down   Subheadings

```




```

What do I expect to find out from reading this article?

```




```

Action   Now read the article.

Result   What have I found out? Write down the *main* ideas (in note form).

```







```

Evaluation   Did I find out what I expected?   Yes   No

                How difficult was the reading?   Hard   OK   Easy

Writer's stance

```

```

Summary

Reading for overview of information

1 Pay attention to the headline, and any bias you detect in it.
2 Look at any subheading to see what it adds to the detail or direction of the article.
3 Check the whole article for any further phrases/extracts that have been highlighted typographically for hints about important detail.

When you go through the above procedure, it means that your first real reading of the article will be focused on the main ideas – it will be **active** reading, not **passive**.

Below are two examples for you to try.

Example 1

> ## GLASGOW'S INDOMITABLE SPIRIT IS ITS ETERNAL STRENGTH
>
> **In many times since the war, Glasgow's mettle has been tested and our people not found wanting**
>
> *Out of two centuries of inequality and heavy blows – warmth and sense of optimism still exists*

? Question

- What do you expect to find out from reading this? (**Answer (1)** on page 35.)

Example 2

> ## IN SEARCH OF THE TRUTH ABOUT MODERN FATHERHOOD
>
> **There are still plenty of failures out there – across every class and in every town. But most men are trying very hard to be the fathers they imagined themselves to be**
>
> *'A great dad can build, a bad dad can stunt, a dreadful dad can ruin'*

? Question

- What discussion do you expect in this article? (**Answer (2)** on page 35.)

Reading paragraphs

Paragraphing is the writer's tool for giving you 'the story' in manageable sections. A new paragraph can signal any of the following:

- the introduction of a new idea
- the contradiction of a previous paragraph
- an additional development of the topic
- an opening of a new point of view in an argument
- a conclusion.

Look at the example below from an article about househusbands.

> *Last week, a report found that there are now in the region of 200,000 househusbands in this country: I am one of them.* Like blue whales, we rarely meet and when we do, we cluster. I know about eight other househusbands, although, to be pedantic about it, most of them are part-timers, splitting the domestic stuff with their partners. And part-time is not full-time; there is a profound difference. I have abandoned my career to raise our son and, perhaps one day, his sibling. When I fill in forms now, under occupation I write 'househusband'.

The topic of this paragraph is that there are now a number of men who stay at home to look after their children.

> *It is difficult being a househusband; certainly more difficult than I had imagined.* The practical aspects of parenting – naps, meals, baths, bedtimes – are well established. None of it is the least bit difficult, once you know how. But a lot of it is boring. And the hours . . . they start when it's dark and cold, and they last for an unreasonable amount of time. There is little time to yourself; no time for mulling over your emails, or surfing the web, or popping out for some pleasure shopping. There's no breakfast and a shower before work. You live and sleep on the shop floor.

The topic of this paragraph is that being a househusband is difficult. The rest of the paragraph lists some of the challenges.

> *When I do get ground down, when it feels really relentless, I have to be reminded that this is not for ever and that I'm travelling emotionally, if not geographically.* I'm learning about myself, developing the patience and sympathy that I never even thought I lacked. Best of all, Jack and I like each other. I'm always pleased to see him. We spend nearly every waking hour together, yet when I'm not with him I miss him. I know what 'poi' and 'sha' mean. Above all, I know in every bone of my body that I will never regret this. I will not lie on my deathbed and think, oh, how I wish I'd spent less time with my son.

The topic of this paragraph is that it is not all gloom and doom. The rest of the paragraph gives the most important plus point.

These three paragraphs have informed you of three steps in the argument about househusbands.

1 There are now a lot of men who are staying at home to look after their children.
2 It is not a particularly easy task.
3 But there are some great compensations.

The advantage of being able to perform this kind of paragraph identification quickly is that it allows you to see the main items without getting bogged down in detail. It takes practice. You could add it to the exercise on page 29. Choose two or three paragraphs, try to identify the topic of each and see how they link together in the argument. Help is available in your ability to spot the obvious linking words – ones that you yourself will be familiar with from your own writing (page 6).

Hints & tips ⭐

Argument *is used here in its academic sense or literary sense – as we have already discussed on page 3. It means the structure or framework of a discussion on a topic.*

Summary

1 Identify the topic of each paragraph.
2 Look at the sequence, the linking, and see how the argument develops.

Reading sentences

Sometimes you have to find your way through a particularly long and complex sentence rather in the same way as you have just learned to look at paragraphs. You have to find out the important or main idea that the sentence contains. As each paragraph has a topic sentence, so a sentence has a **subject**. The subject is the thing or person the sentence is going to tell you about.

Here is a typical long sentence:

> *Feeling that they have failed to be the fathers they hoped – and becoming mildly depressed because of this – modern dads are increasingly avoiding emotional involvement with their children: one quarter said they never talked about personal issues with their child at all.*

What is the subject here, and what are we being told about it?

The first thing you can do to simplify the sentence is to ignore the part between the two dashes – the part in parenthesis. Then you can take out the part after the colon as it is an expansion or example of what is dealt with in the part of the sentence preceding it.

So the sentence becomes:

> *Feeling that they have failed to be the fathers they hoped, modern dads are increasingly avoiding emotional involvement with their children:*

Who is the 'they' referred to in the first few words of the sentence? It has to be 'modern dads', so the **subject** of the sentence is 'modern dads' and we are told that they are avoiding emotional involvement. The important idea therefore is that modern fathers avoid emotional involvement.

The rest of the sentence after the colon gives an example of this (not talking to their children) and the bit in parenthesis, between the two dashes, tells us that the situation has a bad effect on the fathers (they become mildly depressed).

Summary

1 Try to identify the main 'subject' of the sentence.
2 Look at what you are being told about the subject.
3 To simplify the sentence you can temporarily ignore parts in parenthesis, or examples, lists or explanations.

Answers

Answer (1) (page 32)
The article will look at Glaswegians' response to adversity, despite the difficulties (possibly economic) they face.

Answer (2) (page 32)
The article will deal with aspects of fatherhood where the outlook is optimistic, but it will also look at the effect of 'bad' parenting.

Hints & tips

If you become an expert reader and master the skills we have been looking at in this chapter, you will be much more able to find your way through an article on your own, with little (or no) support from questioning on the article. This is the situation you will have to cope with when reading the second passage in the Reading for Understanding, Analysis and Evaluation exam paper.

Chapter 3
Reading for Understanding, Analysis and Evaluation

The work in the previous chapter should enable you to grasp the general subject and argument of a piece of non-fiction prose – an article, or an extract from a longer work. In the exam paper, you are required to show that you can understand the **detail** and the **effectiveness** of the writing you are presented with.

Hints & tips

If you haven't already done so, read the Introduction to this book, because it gives you useful advice on how to use this book effectively.

Exam paper

You will be presented with two pieces of writing that deal with the same topic or theme. There will be questions on one of the passages, and a question (or questions) that ask you to compare the two passages in some way.

There are 30 marks awarded to this exercise, and you have 1 hour 30 minutes to complete it.

The three skills of '**understanding**', '**analysis**' and '**evaluation**' are dependent on each other, and it is perhaps a little artificial to separate them out. For example, in the following paragraph from an article about modern approaches to childhood, the question has **two** parts but the overall answer involves demonstrating all **three** skills.

> And yet our panic about childhood betrays a deep ambivalence, too. Our children are in danger, fattened on fast food, corrupted by commerce, traumatised by testing. And, at the same time, other children are dangerous, malevolent beneath hooded tops, chaotic in the classroom, perilous on the pavements. Before we can have a sensible debate on child-rearing, we need to unpick which of our anxieties truly reflects the reality of the situation.

(?) Question

- Explain what are the two views of childhood stated here, and analyse how these two views are effectively brought to our attention.

The first part of the question is concerned with your **understanding** of the main opposing ideas in the paragraph; the rest of the question asks you to **evaluate** the success of the writing by **analysing** aspect(s) of the language. Thinking about both parts of the question can help you demonstrate that you have fully understood the paragraph.

Analysis

The fact that you have two parallel sentences, one with 'our children are in danger' and the other with 'other children are dangerous', shows that there are two **contrasting** views of children.

The **lists** which follow these statements give us a vivid picture of the number of things adults fear. The **alliteration** in each of the phrases that make up the lists add to the fear. Take the phrase 'traumatised by testing'. Without the alliteration 'testing' could be seen as a fairly neutral word, but linked by sound to 'traumatised' it makes the experience sound quite terrifying.

Understanding

As a result of your analysis you are helped towards your **understanding** of the paragraph, i.e. the gap between these two views has to be taken into account so that what really is worrying about the situation can be debated.

Context

The word 'ambivalence' at the end of the first sentence in the paragraph, which you may not have known the meaning of at first reading, is defined by the text:

> **ambivalence:** *two opposing views, which have to be weighed up against each other*

In other words, the **context** of the word – the rest of the sentence or paragraph in which you find it – helps you to deduce its meaning.

The ability to deduce the meaning of a word from its context lies at the heart of our ability to understand language. As a baby, you learned to understand the word 'milk' because there actually was milk there in front of you. Before you could read, you never looked up a word in the dictionary to see what a word meant. You knew its meaning because of the **context** in which you had heard the word. 'Mind the kerb'; 'go to sleep'; 'please bring me the book' are phrases you 'just knew' because of the place and the objects surrounding you.

It becomes more difficult later in life with abstract ideas, but there are still clues provided by the context. In the following example, 'voracious' is possibly a word you have not seen before.

> *Since the 1990s, this disaster has seen the voracious global fishing system savage 90 per cent of the ocean's largest species – tuna, swordfish and sharks – bringing about an imminent end to the eco-system, the planet and the one billion people who rely on fish for protein.*

From the context – in a sentence that includes words like 'disaster' and 'savage' – it is obvious that 'voracious' means something that is destructive to 90 per cent of large fish.

If you deduced from this that 'voracious' involves vast consumption, you would be very close to its meaning, which is 'extremely hungry' or 'desiring to devour'.

Summary

1 Questions may contain elements of all three aspects of your reading: understanding, analysis and evaluation.
2 These three skills are interdependent: analysis may help you to understand or vice versa. Evaluation should give you an overview of how understanding and analysis work together effectively.
3 The context (the sentence or paragraph surrounding an unfamiliar concept or word) can help you understand it.

Understanding
Understanding the meaning of individual words or key phrases

Understanding is a basic skill that you need whenever you are asked in a question to **explain** something or to **identify** a point or points in the argument.

In both these situations you have to demonstrate that you understand the language of the passage, and to do that you have to understand the meaning of the words or phrases in the lines you are directed to look at. The following is a simple example.

> *The beneficial potential of new media is seldom given much publicity either. Research suggests that computer games can assist children's social and educational development.*

? Question

- Explain what needs to be more fully publicised.

Remember

Whether or not you are reminded explicitly to do so, you must always use your own words when you are giving an explanation.

Your answer has to show that you know what 'beneficial potential' means. The sentence that follows suggests that good results arise from the use of new media, so 'beneficial' must mean 'for the good' in some way, and 'potential' suggests that something 'can' happen or 'has the power' to happen – to bring about improved results in children's development.

Therefore your answer could read something like:

> *The fact that the new media have the possibility of being good for children's development needs to be given more publicity.*

Or, more simply:

> *The new media offer the possibility of being good for children's development.*

You have used the **context** of the sentence to help you understand the meaning of the phrase. This is exactly what you did with the word 'ambivalence' in the previous example on page 37.

Here is an example for you to try from the article on new media.

> *But today's concerns exist in the context of broader adult unease about the proliferation of technology, particularly in the home, and the challenge to adult authority that it represents. The majority of children in the UK now have their own laptop, tablet or smartphone. And they are frequently more competent navigators of the new media than their parents are.*

 Question

- Explain what two things the adults are uneasy about. (**Answer (1)** on page 84.)

Summary 👍

1 Make sure that you tackle the difficult words in a phrase or sentence.
2 Remember that **context** is helpful and can help you to explain how you arrived at a particular meaning.

Identifying points

An important part of demonstrating your understanding of a passage or extract is to be able to recognise the evidence being provided to expand on the topic of a paragraph.

Use the skills we have covered in the previous section to help you express these points in your own words.

Here is a simple example:

> *Since the 1990s, this disaster has seen the voracious global fishing system savage 90 per cent of the ocean's largest species – tuna, swordfish and sharks – bringing about an imminent end to the eco-system, the planet and the one billion people who rely on fish for protein. And if we don't know much about fish in peril because we just don't particularly care – then why*

not? Is it because we 'must' eat fish for our 'essential' Omega 3, otherwise we'll be dead within weeks from nineteenth-century scurvy? Or because fish are Earth's own aliens, no-limbed spooky beings with amoebas for brains? Or because we've more important things to worry about, like unemployment?

(?) Question

- Identify three reasons why we don't care that we eat too much fish.

First you have to isolate the three reasons. The punctuation of a paragraph such as this often helps to clarify where one reason stops and the next begins. The three reasons follow the question '… we just don't particularly care – then why not?'

1 'Is it because we 'must' eat fish for our 'essential' Omega 3, otherwise we'll be dead within weeks from nineteenth-century scurvy?'
2 'Or because fish are Earth's own aliens, no-limbed spooky beings with amoebas for brains?'
3 'Or because we have more important things to worry about, like unemployment?'

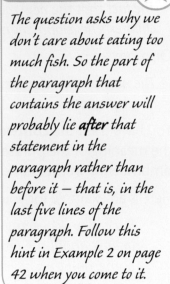

Hints & tips

The question asks why we don't care about eating too much fish. So the part of the paragraph that contains the answer will probably lie **after** that statement in the paragraph rather than before it – that is, in the last five lines of the paragraph. Follow this hint in Example 2 on page 42 when you come to it.

Now try to show that you understand the meaning of each reason.
1 Fish provides necessary items to supplement our diet so that we avoid illness.
2 Fish are not attractive animals so we don't care about them.
3 Other, more important, aspects of our lives don't leave us any room to care about fish.

Hints & tips

In this case the finding of the three reasons is easy, as each is given a separate question. But to write them down, just as they are, lifted from the passage, would not gain any marks.

Try the following two examples:

Example 1

The informal curricular programme in schools is also changing and being given a larger role. Once we would have said this was to promote a rounded education, but now it also helps to hone the skills employers seek. Pursuing private passions through clubs – from the debating society to the magazine committee – has always been part of the lifeblood of a good school. A greater emphasis on civic engagement means volunteering your time: perhaps helping with art in a local primary school or helping with a riding scheme for the disabled. The new buzzword is 'entrepreneurship'. This autumn, students will launch a charity shop. Run by students, it will generate profits for a charity while giving its directors business experience.

(?) Question

- Identify three types of interests covered by a good informal curricular programme which are described in this paragraph. (**Answer (2)** on page 84.)

Example 2

> *The beneficial potential of new media is seldom given much publicity either. Research suggests that computer games can assist children's social and educational development. Young people are using technology to learn and connect with friends across the globe. Nor is the perception of computer games as unremittingly violent accurate, given that the majority of those aimed at children involve imaginative role play.*

(?) Question

- Identify three ways in which the new media benefit children's social and education development. (**Answer (3)** on page 84.)

Summary

1 Remember to use your own words where possible.
2 Use the sentences' structure and/or punctuation as a guide to isolating separate points.

Explaining developments

We have already looked at this idea in Chapter 2 in the sections on **Reading paragraphs** and **Reading sentences** on pages 33–35.

Questions that ask you to **explain** points rather than simply to **identify** them will involve this technique.

You will also need this technique for dealing with questions asking you to take a wider look at the passage(s). These questions could be about:
- the conclusion of an argument or
- the comparison between two passages or
- the necessity to summarise.

Links within a paragraph or sentence

Here, when you are dealing with a section of text, there will be links within the paragraph or sentence that show how the idea is developing.

In the previous section on **Identifying points** we dealt with simple addition: one point + second point + etc.

When explaining the development of an idea, there's usually a more complex relationship between the points. For example:
- an opposition – *but*
- a reason – *because*
- a solution – *therefore*.

Example 1

> *The findings of a survey of more than 2,100 adults suggest that fatherhood is becoming a mild form of depression for the modern-day man, with a grey cloud hanging over it. Many of these men thought of themselves as New Men (with all*

the warm, sensitive emotional capacities that entails) **until**
they became new fathers, which is **why** *they are all the more*
disappointed when they fail to be the sort of dads they expected
and hoped to be. The disappointment and feeling of failure
results *in men shutting down emotionally* **because** *they no*
longer have the old central role in their family and don't know
what other role is available for them.

(?) Question

- Explain how the idea that modern fatherhood is becoming a mild form of depression is developed.

Answer

- Their expectations of what they thought they would be like as fathers– ideal, bonded, caring – have not been realised. **Therefore** their disappointment has caused them to suppress their emotions **because** they don't know how to react.

Example 2
(The first part of the question has been answered for you.)

> *With nearly one million young people unemployed, few*
> *secondary-school age students could be unaware that their*
> *prospects are different from those of their parents. So in schools*
> *'employability' is a focus in itself: academic qualifications count,*
> *but so do an understanding of the job market and the personal*
> *qualities of flexibility, imagination and adaptability. And careers*
> *education is a serious business. Diagnostic online profiling, subject*
> *choices and guidance on applying to university ensure that, in*
> *the final three years of school, the focus is on the long term.*

(?) Question

- Identify the main idea in the topic sentence of this paragraph.

Answer

- Most secondary-school age students recognise that their prospects (for employment) are different from (worse than) those of their parents.

(?) Question

- Explain how the rest of the paragraph develops this idea. (**Answer (4)** on page 85.)

Links between paragraphs

In the context of the whole passage, or a major section of the passage, the tracing of development is important in helping you to recognise the major shifts in the writer's argument. Is the writer presenting conflicting points of view, building a cumulative one-sided case, showing a progression or presenting alternate paragraphs in opposition? Your ability to recognise what is going on is important for your overall understanding and evaluation of the passage(s).

Hints & tips ★

*This requires more than
just simple identification of
points – you are asked to
explain. Therefore, it is the
relationship between the
points that is important.
In the answer, this is dealt
with by using 'therefore'
and 'because' – showing
that there is a causal
relationship between the
two items: the two items
don't exist in isolation from
each other – there is
a cause and therefore
an effect.*

Remember

*Remember to answer
questions using your
own words.*

We have already discussed linking in the chapter on discursive essays (page 6). This is just one example of how your ability to read and analyse other writers' prose helps you in your own attempts to write.

Example 1

Here is a simple example of helpful linking of an argument.

> **Two years ago**, this was my life: I worked in a converted warehouse in Hoxton, east London. It was a bright, young company; the work was brain-achingly demanding and we put in long hours. There were often drinks after work. Weekends consisted of hungover mornings in bed and longer lunches with friends. Resolutions to take more exercise and see more of the insides of theatres/museums were daily broken.

> **Yesterday**, at 5.30 a.m., I was to be found swaying to and fro in the dark, attempting to coax my toddler son back into his cot for another hour's sleep. His cries of 'sha' (lights) and 'poi' (porridge) were a bad omen and I soon conceded. On came the lights and we made our weary way downstairs. At 7 p.m., after almost 14 hours on the go, Jack went to bed. I washed up, watched telly, then went to bed early. This is my life.

> **Last week**, a report found that there are now in the region of 200,000 househusbands in this country: I am one of them …

The words in bold help you to find your way quickly through the writer's argument. In this case it is a really simple sequence.

The first two paragraphs show the contrast between his life then and his life now, leading up to the more general point, which is going to be covered in the information about 'last week's' report.

Example 2

In this next example, the linkage is not as obvious but it is effective in promoting the writer's argument. The important phrases are in bold.

> *You could sum up a year in a hundred different ways. Sport, weather, births, deaths, affairs of state, or the fortunes of a single life. If you are allowed only one choice, though, which headline sticks? As December 2013 descended into hard rain and hail, there was this:* **'Fivefold increase in users of food banks and soup kitchens.'**
>
> *If you didn't pause over* **that statement,** *you are either very young or very lucky. In most of my existence the idea of soup kitchens was confined to grainy photographs from bygone days, or to seasonal appeals for the destitute. Now it is commonplace.* **What was once troubling passes for normal.**
>
> **It has become normal with astonishing speed.** *Wages are depressed while bills rise ever upward. Pensions and savings descend to the level of a lottery. Education, once the route to security, has left us with legions of well-read casual labourers. For those not granted even that promise there is the zero hours contract, the bedroom tax, the abolition of any right to social security and the stigma of poverty.*

Look at how the linking helps you to follow the argument.

The link between the first paragraph and the second is the phrase 'If you didn't pause over that statement …' The words 'that statement' take you back to the previous sentence about 'soup kitchens', and the rest of the paragraph that follows deals with the idea of 'soup kitchens' in the past and in the present.

The link between the second and the third paragraph is contained in the sentence 'It has become normal with astonishing speed'. The word 'normal' picks up the idea of the 'normalisation' of the drastic situation talked of in the paragraph about soup kitchens and the 'astonishing speed' looks forward to what is described in the rest of the third paragraph about the problems caused by the escalation of the present economic situation.

The development of the argument can be traced though the three paragraphs as follows:
1 The rise of soup kitchens is the most important headline of the year.
2 Soup kitchens were a thing of the past, a bad memory, but now they are considered normal again.
3 This has all happened very quickly because of the dire economic situation.

Mastering this skill allows you to pinpoint the important stages in the writer's argument.

> ### Hints & tips ★
> *You may not be asked a question explicitly about linkage, but it is important that you can see this technique in operation as it will help you to deal with the second passage in the exam paper.*

Here is an example for you to tackle.

Example 3

The stakes have never been higher, scientists said. The oceans are becoming increasingly important to global food security. Each year more than a million commercial fishing vessels extract more than 80 million metric tonnes of fish and seafood from the ocean. Up to three billion people rely on the sea for a large share of their protein, especially in the developing world.

Those demands are only projected to grow. 'If you look at where food security has to go between now and 2030 we have to start looking at the ocean. We have to start looking at the proteins coming from the sea,' said Valerie Hickey, an environmental scientist at the World Bank.

That makes it all the more crucial to crack down on illegal and unregulated fishing, which is sabotaging efforts to build sustainable seafood industries. Two-thirds of the fish taken on the high seas are from stocks that are already dangerously depleted – far more so than in those parts of the ocean that lie within 200 miles of the shore and are under direct national control.

? Question

- Identify the links in the writer's argument. (**Answer (5)** on page 85.)

Answer (5) on page 85.

Summary

1 When you are asked to explain, it means you have to do more than just identify.
2 Linking words and phrases (and sentences) help to signpost stages in the writer's thought, and therefore help your explanation.
3 Remember it is still important to put as much of your answer as you can in your own words.

Hints & tips ★

Look out for repetition of words or ideas, and watch for the words that create stages in the argument – the signposts mentioned on page 6.

Use of examples/illustrations and anecdotes

Writers often use examples and anecdotes to clarify abstract points in their argument. This helps the reader because it takes the abstract idea and presents it in human terms. It is often why serious articles about, for example, political dilemmas use what are called 'human interest' stories. Such articles are attempting to clarify a situation by using the description of an actual human experience, and they are often trying to engage your sympathies on a personal as well as an intellectual level.

Example 1

I visited a Trussell Trust foodbank this week, in Hackney in East London, no more than a three-minute walk from a pleasant green complete with upmarket cafés and a specialist Italian deli. It is a sight at once heartening and shaming. Heartening because it is good to see that people are still willing to give up time, money and effort to care with great sensitivity and respect for those they have never met. Shaming because, in global terms, 'we are a wealthy country', and in a wealthy country people should not go hungry.

The pity of it is inescapable. I saw a man take home a couple of carrier bags filled with the most basic kind of basics: tinned sausages, a can of soup, a packet of pasta. All decent enough, each allocation calculated for balance by nutritionists. Except that you and I would not want to live on that for three days, which is how long it has to last.

In this example the abstract ideas of 'shame' and 'in a wealthy country people should not grow hungry' are given more emotional impact by the author's description of a real person who is reduced to plastic bags of 'basics'. It induces the 'pity' he is trying to raise in his readers.

Example 2

Without doubt we humans are changing, just as we changed centuries ago with the print revolution. But research into the effects of new technology has always been contradictory.

People once fretted over what the telephone and the radio would do to us. In 1835, the American Annals of Education declared that 'the perpetual reading' of novels 'inevitably operates to exclude thought and, in the youthful mind, to stint the opening mental faculties, by favouring unequal development: no-one can have time for reflection, who reads at this rapid rate'.

(?) Question

- This example works in the same way as the previous one. Comment on its effectiveness. (**Answer (6)** on page 85.)

Example 3

This anecdote occurs in an article criticising the way in which emails and mobile phones have spread through all aspects of our lives. The writer does not use either of these.

> *The only time I might conceivably have needed a mobile phone outside the house was when I once turned my car over in the Irish mountains and was trapped inside the vehicle for a while. When a passer-by did finally try to use a phone, however, it didn't work, since the mountains were too high. Hanging upside down like a gigantic bat, my chest crushed painfully against the airbag, I felt quietly vindicated.*

(?) Question

- Explain how this anecdote helps to support the writer's stance about mobile phones. (**Answer (7)** on page 85.)

Effectiveness of a conclusion

This kind of question is quite commonly used to check that you have followed the argument of the paragraph, or – more commonly – a whole passage, and that you can appreciate the writer's skill in reaching an effective conclusion.

A good conclusion to an article normally achieves one, or both, of the following:
1 It should tie up the writer's argument (the ideas), making clear his or her stance/point of view.
2 It should relate to the rest of the article, by reminding us of important points, by choice of language or by structural techniques.

Although the following piece (only 331 words) is shorter than passages you will get in the exam, it is enough to illustrate the idea of an effective conclusion.

Example 1

> **Hunger for success**
>
> *It is interesting to see a new Department for Education study urging universities to consider lowering entry requirements for state-school pupils. It argues that when state-educated pupils have the same grades as those educated at fee-paying schools, on average they go on to attain better degrees, and are also less likely to drop out.*
>
> *These state-school students have to fight against unfair odds to get into universities, a battle that these days incorporates everything from limited educational opportunities and lack of financial*

support to huge fees and loans. The whole process looks unfair, exhausting and economically terrifying, and that's even when everything goes to plan. Saying that, what this study suggests is that, given half a chance, many students from the fabled 'wrong side of town' have what it takes to excel at university level, even to surpass some of their more privileged peers. It would appear that the determination required to keep hacking away, fighting through the thickets and briars of a disadvantaged start, the intelligence and strong will that keeps a person focused and on track stays with them during their university years.

Could this be where the disadvantaged have a bizarre kind of advantage? For all the love and good intentions that may be around them, the support and opportunities too often aren't – so they have no choice but to be self-starting, self-motivated, their own raw version of self-made.

Take this attitude into a university setting, where self-reliance is king, and it becomes akin to having a superpower. Getting bored, becoming demotivated, giving up, dropping out – to the disadvantaged, self-made university student, these options would be unthinkable.

The thought that, once at university, such students tend not only to do well, but disproportionately so, is encouraging – which in turn lends weight to the argument for helping more of them do likewise, by the simple act of lowering university requirements to a fair and realistic level. Far from being reverse discrimination, this would be anti-discrimination, ultimately benefiting all.

(?) Question

- Evaluate the final paragraph's effectiveness as a conclusion to the article.

Answer

- The last paragraph provides an effective conclusion to the ideas of the passage as it takes into account the two main ideas of the passage: that entry to university education is unfair to state-educated pupils (although there might ultimately be some advantage in this for them); and that the system ought to be reformed to get rid of inequalities.
- The last sentence is particularly effective in summing up in a few words the fairness of a reformed system, with the climax being the notion that it would benefit everyone.

This answer looks mainly at ideas, but the technique of building to a climax in the last sentence is also mentioned.

Example 2

I am not connected

I shall soon be the only EMV (email virgin) left in the country. I have never sent an email, though I've occasionally cheated and asked my teenage son to do so for me. Nor have I ever used the internet. I am no more capable of going online than I am of getting to Saturn. I don't know how to text. I do have a mobile phone, but it's immobile. I never take it out of the house, for fear of triggering some ridiculous trend in which a horde of people march down the street bawling into these sinister little gadgets. If you allowed people to use mobile phones in public, you might end up being forced to listen to them on trains and in cafés, asking noisily whether the invoices have arrived. The prospect is too appalling to contemplate. The only time I might conceivably have needed a mobile phone outside the house was when I once turned my car over in the Irish mountains and was trapped inside the vehicle for a while. When a passer-by did finally try to use a phone, however, it didn't work, since the mountains were too high. Hanging upside down like a gigantic bat, my chest crushed painfully against the airbag, I felt quietly vindicated.

Nowadays, however, protest is most definitely what my email virginity has become. I am living proof that all this frenetic, mostly vacuous, communication is quite superfluous. We all survived without it before it started, and I personally have survived without it ever since. If people really want to contact me they write. If they can't be bothered, or have forgotten how to do it, that's their problem.

? Question

- Explain how the last paragraph makes an effective conclusion to the article. (**Answer (8)** on page 85.)

Summary

1 Look at how the ideas have been followed through to the ending, clarifying the writer's stance or point of view.
2 Consider the techniques the writer uses to emphasise his or her stance, or to provide a climax to or a final twist in the article.

Hints & tips ★

Look for repetition in the last paragraph of words, phrases or imagery that have occurred earlier in the passage — often at the very beginning. Sometimes the title or heading of the passage is echoed in the conclusion.

Analysis

We have seen already how understanding, analysis and evaluation are inextricably mixed together, but on some occasions you will be asked to comment on or evaluate the effectiveness of certain features or techniques employed by the writer.

There are several ways in which you could be asked to approach these questions. For example:

- By referring to at least one example, analyse how the writer's use of imagery …
- By referring to examples, analyse how the writer's use of word choice and sentence structure …
- By referring to at least two features of language, analyse … You should refer in your answer to such features as sentence structure, word choice, tone …
- By referring to at least two features of language, analyse …

In the first case, you have no choice, you have to analyse the feature mentioned – in this case, imagery.

In the second case, you have no choice, you have to analyse the features mentioned – in this case, word choice and sentence structure. This is a **closed** list – you can't choose anything else.

In the third case, you can analyse any feature you think is effective. The list you are given is an **open** list – you may accept the suggestions offered to you, but you could choose any language feature you think is effective.

In the fourth case, you can again choose any language feature you think is effective, but you are given no support, so you should have a 'tick list' in your head to remind you of the kind of features you might be looking for.

In the following section we are going to look at the following items on that 'tick list' which you will find useful in answering such questions:

1 word choice
2 imagery
3 sentence structure
4 tone.

Word choice

This is really a very simple technique to get to grips with. The question you have to ask yourself is **why** a writer has chosen one particular word to describe someone or something, rather than any of the other words that have a similar meaning. English is a rich language – it has twice the vocabulary of French, for example – and has many **synonyms** (words of the same meaning). Purists in language will tell you that there is no such thing as a synonym – and they are right – but for our purposes we will stick with the common definition.

Take 'friendly', 'chummy' and 'comradely'. All three of these could describe a comfortable relationship. They have the same 'meaning'. The technical word for this is **denotation**. Any English speaker would recognise the kind of person being described.

But there is a difference between the effect of each of the three words. Each of them *implies* something different about the relationship. This further implication is technically called **connotation**.

The table below shows the denotations and connotations of the three words.

Word	Denotation	Connotation
Friendly	Close relationship	A fairly neutral description of people who find pleasure in each other's company.
Chummy	Close relationship	Suggests an intimacy shared between two people who are close and comfortable in each other's company, perhaps for a long time – since childhood maybe.
Comradely	Close relationship	Suggests a closeness coming from mutual support – possibly belonging to a team or an organisation.

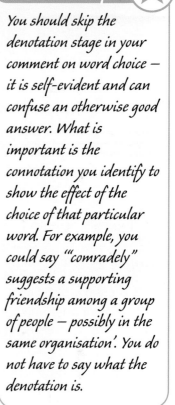

Hints & tips

You should skip the denotation stage in your comment on word choice – it is self-evident and can confuse an otherwise good answer. What is important is the connotation you identify to show the effect of the choice of that particular word. For example, you could say "comradely" suggests a supporting friendship among a group of people – possibly in the same organisation'. You do not have to say what the denotation is.

Writers are careful in their choice of words – it is their profession, after all. We should do them the honour of appreciating the effects their choices have on us. Connotations are sometimes hard to pin down – you know what effect the words have, but you can't quite explain it. The larger the vocabulary you have, the more likely it is that you can find the words you need to describe the connotations, and that goes back to the amount you read or listen to. Constant practice is the best way.

Let's look again at one of the examples used at the start of this chapter to explore the connotations of words.

Example 1

> *And yet our panic about childhood betrays a deep ambivalence, too. Our children are in danger, fattened on fast food, corrupted by commerce, traumatised by testing. And, at the same time, other children are dangerous, malevolent beneath hooded tops, chaotic in the classroom, perilous on the pavements. Before we can have a sensible debate on child-rearing, we need to unpick which of our anxieties truly reflects the reality of the situation.*

The most obvious examples of the writer choosing words to make an effect are the ones where she is talking about the negative views of childhood. The list of possibilities is quite extensive.

- '**fattened**' suggests that the children are likely to become obese, almost like pigs which are 'fattened' especially for market.
- '**fast food**' suggests cheap, not particularly nutritious food, not prepared with care and therefore not healthy.
- '**corrupted**' – the idea of corruption is strong, as if the children are part of the criminal world already.

- '**commerce**' possibly suggests that they are part of a society that buys and sells anything for profit.
- '**traumatised**' suggests that the children have actually been wounded, perhaps not physically, but certainly mentally.
- '**testing**' suggests an unpleasant experience with scary exams.
- '**malevolent**' suggests that children can be seen almost as bad spirits, out to cause harm deliberately.
- '**hooded**' suggests something hidden, and therefore mysterious, threatening and dangerous.

Hints & tips

The word 'suggests' is used in these answers to show that you are moving from the reference (for which you get no marks) to the connotative area of the word you have chosen to deal with.

Hints & tips

You would not choose anything like this number of words for comment. The easiest words to deal with are probably 'fattened', 'corrupted', 'traumatised' and 'hooded'. You should take note of the number of marks available for your answer and assume that you stand a chance of making at least 1 mark for each comment. Remember that you gain no marks for simply quoting the word itself. The mark is in the comment.

Now look at the following example and answer the question that follows.

Example 2

> *There's also the matter of not being bothered enough to think of anything else to eat in the face of a sumptuously juicy salmon steak fizzing away under the grill, to be served with a drizzle of virgin olive oil and a splash of the zingiest lemon – yum! For me, a world without fish is a world where there's nowt for tea. I write as someone who eats fish three times a week, who hasn't eaten meat since 1983 and has been resolutely adolescent on the subject ever since.*

 Question

- Analyse how the writer, by her word choice, makes her eating of fish sound attractive. (**Answer (9)** on pages 85–86.)

Hints & tips

This question is not quite typical of the question you may actually be asked in the exam. It would be more usual to find 'word choice' as one of a number of techniques you are offered for comment. You could also comment on 'word choice' in an answer to a question asking you to analyse the language of a particular sentence or paragraph.

*'Language' covers a number of techniques besides word choice, including **imagery**, **sentence structure** and **tone**, which will be discussed in the rest of this section on Analysis.*

Now look at the following example:

Example 3

> *It is difficult being a househusband; certainly more difficult than I had imagined. The practical aspects of parenting – naps, meals, baths, bedtimes – are well established. None of it is the least bit difficult, once you know how. But a lot of it is boring. And the hours … they start when it's dark and cold, and they last for an unreasonable amount of time. There is little time to yourself; no time for mulling over your emails, or surfing the web, or popping out for some pleasure shopping. There's no breakfast and a shower before work. You live and sleep on the shop floor.*

(?) Question

- By referring to at least two examples, analyse how the writer gives the impression that being a househusband is time-consuming. (**Answer (10)** on page 86.)

Summary

1 The more extensive your vocabulary, the more easily will you be able to express the connotations of the words you choose to examine.
2 The more you read, the more you will extend your vocabulary.

Imagery

Imagery can refer to pictures or photographs. It is also a technical term used in the analysis of language. The following passage, although it paints a picture and is very descriptive, does not contain any imagery. You could make valid comments on the word choice, but not on imagery.

> *Seven great swans flew overhead, snow-plumaged travellers from the far north who knew the glacial winds of the tundra and the sunny waters of Andalusia. The sun shone on the snow white heads as they swept across the blue-arched sky; then they were gone, with a far carrying swoosh of wings. They had passed over a Glasgow suburb only fifteen minutes before, flying high and strong in the familiar cold, unheard, unseen, eager to splash and dip their beaks in the cold water of the loch beyond Laverock Knowe.*

Imagery in its technical sense has many divisions, but here we are concerned with the following more common ones:
- simile
- metaphor
- personification
- symbolism.

Simile

Similes tend to be easier to spot because they always have a 'like' or an 'as', but they are not necessarily easy to explain. Take the very simple, rather clichéd, example below.

Example 1

> *The messenger ran like the wind.*

If you were asked to analyse the effect of this simile, you could say:

Answer

- The simile gives the impression of the messenger's speed, as the wind is seen as a powerful force that can reach great speeds.

An answer such as 'the messenger runs very fast' would only be giving the meaning of the phrase, not its effect.

In the next extract, taken from a passage about girls and sport, there are two examples of simile, both of which help us to visualise a situation, i.e. they transmit to us an image, making the writer's point more effective.

Example 2

> *It happened overnight. One minute, I was flying down the wing like a character out of 'Bunty'*, my only worry in life that I would lose control of the ball and thus let down our captain Caroline 'Caz' Johnson, a girl who seriously demanded to be impressed. The next, I was a 'Jackie'** photo-strip, obsessed with frosted lipstick and whether my hair looked like Siobhan's out of 'Bananarama'.*
>
> *After this, there was no way back. Reluctant to run or indeed make sudden movements of any kind, I was soon dropped from the hockey team. PE lessons, meanwhile, became a convoluted exercise in avoidance – and not only for me. The slothfulness spread among us girls like a contagion. Cross-country runs began with a truculent jog until we were out of sight of the teachers, at which point we would repair to the nearest newsagent for sweets and a Coke.*

* 'Bunty' was a magazine for girls at the pre-teen stage – now out of print.

** 'Jackie' was a photo-magazine for teenage girls – also now out of print.

The two similes in this paragraph are:
- 'I was flying down the wing like a character out of "Bunty"'.
- 'The slothfulness spread among us girls like a contagion.'
- 'I was flying down the wing like a character out of "Bunty"' is a simile in which the writer compares herself to a character out of 'Bunty' – suggesting that her role models then were the kind of sporty heroines to be found in a magazine such as 'Bunty', which was aimed at pre-teen girls.

⑦ Question

- Comment on the second simile about 'slothfulness'. (**Answer (11)** on page 86.)

Example 3

> *Last week, a report found that there are now in the region of 200,000 househusbands in this country: I am one of them. Like blue whales, we rarely meet and when we do, we cluster. I know about eight other househusbands, although, to be pedantic about it, most of them are part-timers, splitting the domestic stuff with their partners. And part-time is not full-time; there is a profound difference. I have abandoned my career to raise our son and, perhaps one day, his sibling. When I fill in forms now, under occupation I write 'househusband'.*

? Question

- Analyse how the simile in this paragraph helps to emphasise the numbers of househusbands. (**Answer (12)** on page 86.)

Metaphor

A metaphor is the most powerful (and magical) device in the language. If you can learn to appreciate its strength and beauty, it doesn't really matter whether you pass the exam or not – you are a more enlightened person!

Metaphor goes one step further than simile:

- **Simile** says something is *like* something – her home is like a prison.
- **Metaphor** says something *is* something – her home is a prison.

The first of these statements can be true – her home has bolts and bars, high fences, etc.

The second of these statements is not actually true – her home is not one of Her Majesty's prison buildings. But it suggests that some attributes of both home and prison are shared. Some of the connotations of prison are isolation, oppression, being trapped – not necessarily just physical bolts and bars. The metaphor fuses the concepts of 'prison' and 'home' together to make an entirely new concept. It is more powerful than the simile because it opens up many more possibilities – psychological as well as physical. It really creates a new concept – a prison/home.

Think about the following metaphor:

> *In the wind the men clung on to the big, black, circular birds of their umbrellas.*

The two concepts of 'big, black birds' and '(black) umbrellas' are being compared and condensed into a new visual concept suggesting, among other things, that the umbrellas are now animate beings and have a life of their own. The metaphor exists in the overlap between the two connotational areas – the one surrounding 'black birds' and the one surrounding 'umbrellas'.

The process can be illustrated in graphic form in a Venn diagram – this helps anyone whose mind works spatially, rather than abstractly.

Hints & tips ★

A number of the questions throughout the Analysis section of this book are much narrower and more specific than the questions you may get in the exam. In a typical exam question, you might be asked specifically about word choice or imagery, etc.; but it is equally likely that the question would ask 'by referring to at least two features of language…' It is on these occasions that you have to remind yourself of the features of language discussed here.

CONNOTATIONAL IDEAS

METAPHORICAL AREA

Try disentangling the following example – which is a mixture of simile and metaphor – just for fun!

> *The umbrella suddenly bellied out, the spokes tore through the soaking cover; the wind danced its tatters; it wrangled above us in the wind like a ruined mathematical bird. We tried to tug it down: an unseen new spoke sprang through its ragged ribs.*

The following example is a more typical one to try. It is from an article about the difficulties facing children of the twenty-first century.

Example 1

> *But that's not how it is for my kids, and it's not how it is for most kids these days, either: because most of us parents are still largely in control, still mostly rowing our boats, still on the whole steering our children through life's waters and making sure they know what matters in life.*
>
> *Being a kid has never been so good; I feel excited with my children, and for my children, that they're growing up where they are, and when they are: and I believe in them, and in their generation.*

As far as I can see, there's a lot more honey than poison in the cocktail that is childhood in the twenty-first century: and my kids, and all the other kids I know, are the sweeter and more promising for it.

There are a number of metaphors in this extract:

- 'rowing our boats'
- 'steering our children through life's waters'
- 'more honey than poison in the cocktail'.

The first two of these could be put together, because they are both concerned with the idea of boats and water. It is, in fact, an **extended metaphor**. But you can deal with the items separately, or together.

The metaphor 'rowing our boats … steering our children through life's waters' pictures life as being like a sea that needs to be negotiated. It emphasises the parents being in control of the way their children are growing up through life, just as a captain of a boat steers it in the right direction.

This analysis shows how the metaphor works, because it deals with the **figurative** element, the image of the sea/boats/water, and relates it to children's **literal** growing up under the guidance of their parents.

(?) Question

- Analyse the contribution of the honey/poison metaphor to the picture of twenty-first century children's lives. (**Answer (13)** on page 86.)

Hints & tips ★

In dealing with metaphors, you should:

✓ *Show how the words used metaphorically help to enlarge or refine your idea of what is being described (a house, a bat, a child's life).*

✓ *Show the link between the literal (or denotational) meaning of the words used in the metaphor (prison, bits of umbrella, life's waters) and the figurative effect — caused among other things by the fusing of the two concepts.*

Here is another example from a different article on the difficulties facing children of the twenty-first century.

Example 2

Childhood has always been a disputed territory, its true geography quickly forgotten as we grow older, replaced by an adult-imagined universe. But there appears to be a growing consensus that childhood today is in a peculiarly parlous state.

⑦ Question

- Analyse the writer's use of imagery in these lines. (**Answer (14)** on pages 86–87.)

Examples 3 and 4 (below) are from the passage about sustainable fishing.

Example 3

> *No, we don't care about fish because we don't know anything about fish or how they came to be sizzling on our plates. Plundering shoals in supermarkets, we are ill-informed innocents at best, consumptive zombies at worst: inadvertently slicing the kitchen knife through the cast of* Finding Nemo *in front of our weeping children, who may never see their own offspring shriek like seagulls at a gigantic skate's rectangular mouth grimacing through an aquarium wall.*

⑦ Question

- Analyse how the imagery in this paragraph helps the writer to make her point effectively. (**Answer (15)** on page 87.)

Example 4

> *Since the 1990s, this disaster has seen the voracious global fishing system savage 90 per cent of the ocean's largest species – tuna, swordfish and sharks – bringing about an imminent end to the eco-system, the planet and the one billion people who rely on fish for protein.*

⑦ Question

- Analyse the imagery in this paragraph. (**Answer (16)** on page 87.)

Summary

1 Identify or quote the metaphor you are dealing with.
2 Show how the literal and the figurative come together to create an effect.
3 Say what the effect is.

Personification

Personification is really just another kind of metaphor (a 'subset' for those who are mathematically inclined). In personification, some thing or animal is given human attributes. For example, 'The river babbled happily, chuckling over the stones', is a simple use of personification. What is gained by using this sentence rather than simply 'The river flowed over the stones making small noises'? The river, not being a person, cannot either 'babble happily' or 'chuckle' (these are human actions) – but the feeling of happiness and serenity (which are among the connotations of the words) is transferred to the scene by regarding the river as a friendly entity.

Look at the first example, which is the conclusion to the article on page 54 on girls and sport.

Example 1

They need to transmit their excitement, their satisfaction, their sense of liberation and empowerment.

When I think back to the 'Bananarama' days, my hair crisp with Sun-In and Wella gel, it is this flimsiness that pains me most, the sense that I would only be noticed, be found attractive, if I was a blonde smile in stretch jeans. I can't deny that in my nylon hockey skirt and clumpy studded boots, my knees covered in mud and my sweaty fringe in my eyes, I felt that I looked too substantial, too challenging. And that feeling stayed with me for years, long after my hockey stick had been laid to rest in the attic.

How I wish I'd known then what I know now, which is that energy, zest and, above all, strength are twice as attractive as a pampered skin and at least three times as enduring.

(?) Question

- One example of imagery is 'a blonde smile in stretch jeans'. Comment on this metaphor for yourself. (**Answer (17)** on page 87.)

The other example of imagery – 'long after my hockey stick had been laid to rest' – can be dealt with as a metaphor. It is also an example of personification. It doesn't matter which heading you analyse it under – either would be possible – but because this section is on personification, the answer here deals with it as personification.

The hockey stick is being seen as an animate object – a human being – which is 'laid to rest' in the way that you would bury a dead relative.

It suggests that the hockey stick was an old friend, but it had come to the end of its useful life, and was 'buried' in the attic. It is effective in showing how the writer looks back on her sporting life with some affection, and perhaps wishes that she had not so easily given up hockey.

This example is from an article about food phonies and their love of gastroculture.

Example 2

> Gastroculture has a lot to answer for. It has monopolised television schedules. It has spawned live events and even muscled its way into music festivals via gourmet food trucks and VIP dining tickets.

(?) Question

- In what way does personification in this paragraph help promote the writer's critical view of gastroculture? (**Answer (18)** on page 87.)

Symbolism

This concept is related to imagery, but has a much wider significance and a more general application – not just in language, but in art, film and collective culture.

Symbols do not have to have a context in a piece of writing to be effective. A red rose is a symbol, whether it is a physical rose, a virtual rose, a drawing or a photograph of a rose, or the use of the word 'rose'. In the culture of Western Europe it is recognised as a symbol for love.

Literary symbolism, whether in a novel, short story, film or a piece of journalism, is created by the writer specifically to carry an attitude,

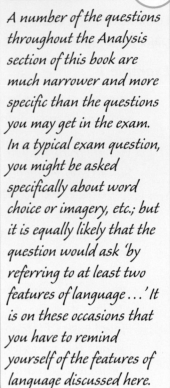

Hints & tips ⭐

A number of the questions throughout the Analysis section of this book are much narrower and more specific than the questions you may get in the exam. In a typical exam question, you might be asked specifically about word choice or imagery, etc.; but it is equally likely that the question would ask 'by referring to at least two features of language …' It is on these occasions that you have to remind yourself of the features of language discussed here.

an emotion or a concept. In *The Cone-Gatherers* the tree and its disease becomes symbolic of Duror's descent into evil. In *Sunset Song*, the standing stones become symbolic of the old ways, Scotland, the land …

In a short article or extract it is not often possible to develop anything of a symbolic nature, but the article we have already looked at on househusbands offers a small example.

Example 1

(Second paragraph of the article on househusbands.)

> *Yesterday, at 5.30 a.m., I was to be found swaying to and fro in the dark, attempting to coax my toddler son back into his cot for another hour's sleep. His cries of 'sha' (lights) and 'poi' (porridge) were a bad omen and I soon conceded. On came the lights and we made our weary way downstairs.*

(And this is the conclusion.)

> *We spend nearly every waking hour together, yet when I'm not with him I miss him. I know what 'poi' and 'sha' mean. Above all, I know in every bone of my body that I will never regret this. I will not lie on my deathbed and think, oh, how I wish I'd spent less time with my son.*

⑦ Question

- What effect does the writer create by his use of the repeated words 'poi' and 'sha' in this article?

Answer

- It is probably true to say that 'poi' and 'sha' have become symbolic of his understanding relationship with his son. It is effective in showing the depth of emotion contained in the intimate domestic detail the symbol is based on.

Sentence structure

Questions on sentence structure require more than just giving the meaning of the sentence. You must talk about the effect of the structure. Does it:

- clarify?
- dramatise?
- balance/contrast ideas?
- shock?

In order to tackle these sentences you should be thinking of at least four possibilities:

1 punctuation
2 length of sentence
3 use of climax or anti-climax
4 repetition (both in sentences and in other contexts).

Hints & tips

You should learn these lists so that you can apply each to any sentence structure you are asked about: it is very likely that one of these techniques will be used in the extract.

Punctuation

You should know the various functions of the main punctuation marks in English:

- full stop (.)
- comma (,)
- semi-colon (;)
- colon (:)
- exclamation mark (!)
- question mark (?)
- inverted commas ('x').

The main purpose of punctuation is to help the reader to understand the sentence. Some of the possible uses are:

- Full stops tell you when one point has been finished.
- An exclamation mark will help you to recognise the tone of a sentence.
- A colon may signal an explanation which you need.
- Semi-colons may provide you with a balancing point in a sentence, either a parallel or a contrast.
- Brackets, pairs of dashes and pairs of commas may indicate a parenthesis.
- Inverted commas may mean quotation, or a title, or they may cast doubt on the truthfulness of the words they highlight.

Hints & tips

A few common errors to do with punctuation:

- Commas do not, on their own, 'do' anything. They may help to mark out something that is already happening in a sentence.
- A single dash may create a pause or allow the addition of an important or dramatic idea – but one dash is not a parenthesis. A parenthesis requires a pair of something: dashes, commas or brackets.

Example 1

> For Rosie and her pals, friendship is hugely important: she and her little gang meet every week or so at someone's house for a pizza and a DVD (another encounter with the small screen) but, hey, they love it. They chat. They giggle. They enjoy one another's company. They can communicate, and communicate well. They make allowances for one another. They share a joke.

Punctuation of these sentences helps to clarify the writer's attitude to her daughter and her friends.

In the first sentence:

- The colon after 'friendship is hugely important' introduces an example of how that friendship works.
- The parenthesis reminds us of the part of the article, earlier in the passage, that suggests that children spend too long with computers and phones.
- The informality of the structure 'but, hey, they love it' is appropriate for a paragraph describing children's behaviour – it echoes their methods of communication.
- The series of short sentences all beginning with 'They' shows how co-operatively her daughter's friends work together.
- The repetition of the word 'communicate' makes that the most important benefit they share.

Obviously you would not be expected to give such a lengthy answer as this, but in this short passage there are several of the common usages of punctuation.

Example 2

> *'Imagine a world without fish.' So runs the simple tag-line for*
> *The End of the Line, a documentary film about fish and how*
> *there literally won't be any left in 2048 due to over-fishing and all*
> *of its deadly friends: industry ruthlessness, merciless profiteering,*
> *governmental short-sightedness, consumer apathy, general*
> *ignorance and outright contempt for the spectrum of marine life*
> *by the majority of human beings.*

The colon after 'all of its deadly friends' introduces a list of the 'deadly friends' of over-fishing. The length of the list shows how many and varied are the enemies of fish stocks, and how likely they are in combination to end up in 'a world without fish' – the important topic sentence. The list builds up to a climax, saving the most important item for last, and the last item is much longer than the rest – 'general ignorance and outright contempt for the spectrum of marine life by the majority of human beings'. Basically the list ends up accusing the reader of being responsible for the depletion of fish stocks.

Example 3

> *Employment is one thing; finding fulfilment and making a*
> *worthwhile contribution to society is another. Whatever their*
> *immediate job prospects, and the difficulties that they will face,*
> *I think that the young people I meet are imaginative, tenacious,*
> *versatile and well-grounded. If our future is in their hands, then I*
> *am optimistic.*

(?) Question

- Analyse the effect of punctuation in these lines in contributing to the strength of this concluding paragraph. (**Answer (19)** on page 87.)

> ### Hints & tips ⭐
>
> You should identify the sentence you are writing about. Sometimes there are two lists quite close together in the passage, so to avoid confusion, use quotes. You don't need to quote the whole sentence or list – the line reference will do, or the opening and closing words.
> Lists are easy to identify, but you must say what the effect of the list is – does it climax in something exciting, for example? Or does it suggest monotonous sameness? Or does it suggest an infinity or an infinite variety of items?

Sentence length

Really there are only two possible comments to make – either the sentence is 'long' or it is 'short'.

Commenting on a sentence's great length on its own is very unlikely to be helpful: there will be more important features, possibly statement and explanation or expansion; parenthetical detail marked by brackets or dashes; lengthy informative lists – the length of the sentence is purely incidental.

A short sentence is more likely to create an obvious effect in a piece of writing than a long one. A short sentence can be:

- dramatic
- declarative
- climactic
- summative.

In each case, a short sentence can be effective in serving the writer's purposes.

Example 1

The other day I was kicked out of a ladies' lavatory.

(The rest of the article discusses the problems caused for a parent who is of the opposite sex from his young child, and which public lavatory to use.)

Obviously this is an example of a dramatic short sentence, its effect being to jolt us into reading what comes next.

Example 2

Whatever their immediate job prospects, and the difficulties that they will face, I think that the young people I meet are imaginative, tenacious, versatile and well-grounded. If our future is in their hands, then I am optimistic.

The last short sentence 'If our … optimistic' could be described as 'declarative': it makes a strong statement that is sure of its ground and does not expect any opposition.

Example 3

Still, the shame is bearable if the alternative is you or your family going hungry. What has become of us, when that is the choice we offer our fellow citizens: dignity or food? And this in our wealthy, wealthy country.

The last short sentence 'And … country' provides a climax to the writer's disapproval of food banks.

Starting the sentence with 'And' emphasises the importance of what the writer is saying. He doesn't just tack it on to the previous sentence in what would be considered a more conventionally 'correct' way. By separating it from its parent sentence the writer forces us to take note of it.

Example 4

> *Yesterday, at 5.30 a.m., I was to be found swaying to and fro in the dark, attempting to coax my toddler son back into his cot for another hour's sleep… At 7 p.m., after almost 14 hours on the go, Jack went to bed. I washed up, watched telly, then went to bed early. This is my life.*

The final short sentence 'This is my life' is summative – it parcels all the long hours he has spent looking after his son into one small phrase that contains it all. The sentence could be described also as anti-climactic, or perhaps even climactic, depending on how you feel about children.

Use of climax and anti-climax

These features are fairly self-explanatory. All that you have to remember is that they present possible areas for comment on sentence structure.

You may be asked specifically to comment on climax or anti-climax, but you should be aware that, when asked to comment on the effectiveness of a sentence, this is a technique worth looking for because its effect is usually fairly easy to describe. The specific word or phrase could be the last item in a list, the last sentence or phrase in a sequence or the last sentence or phrase in a paragraph.

- Example 2 on page 64 shows how climax operates in a list.
- Example 4 above shows the climax of a paragraph.
- Example 3 on page 64 gives an example of climax at the end of an article.

Repetition

Although we are dealing with this under sentence structure, repetition can be effective in many structures. It is not exclusively a feature within a **sentence**. It can be found in **paragraphs** or **complete articles**.

Repetition in the structure of a paragraph

Look at this example from an article entitled 'Have we poisoned childhood?'

Example

> *Too much TV. Bombarded with adverts. Too scared to go outside. Too much fat and sugar. Easily accessed internet pornography. Pressure at school. Mum and Dad both at work. Too many computer games. Too many celebrities to copy, or pity, or aspire to. Too much stuff. Endless piles of stuff.*

In this paragraph the repetition of 'Too' throughout is effective in indicating all the 'excess' heaped on the twenty-first-century child.

Repetition in the structure of a whole article

Example

(Second paragraph in the article.)

> *So, presumably, we are nightmare parents, raising a nightmare generation on a poisonous cocktail of junk food, marketing, over-competitive schooling and electronic entertainment.*

(Last paragraph.)

> *As far as I can see, there's a lot more honey than poison in the cocktail that is childhood in the twenty-first century: and my kids, and all the other kids I know, are the sweeter and more promising for it.*

When you see the second paragraph from the passage, the repetition of the image of the 'poisoned cocktail' in the last paragraph helps you to understand how the passage has developed an argument from 'poison' to 'honey', which shows that the 'bad' aspects of childhood are not necessarily the whole story.

Repetition in general, in all its aspects, is an effective structural tool in language. We learn very young the effect of repetition of sound in the form of rhyme and rhythm; and the effect of the repetition of patterns of words in choruses in children's stories; and the effect of the magic of 'three'. The use of repetition in adult writing may be more subtle but it can have powerful effects.

Repetition of sound

Repetition of sound in the form of alliteration is familiar to us as a feature of poetry, but it is also a part of the prose writer's technique.

Example

> *Our children are in danger, fattened on fast food, corrupted by commerce, traumatised by testing. And, at the same time, other children are dangerous, malevolent beneath hooded tops, chaotic in the classroom, perilous on the pavements.*

Here the alliteration in 'fattened on fast food', for example, draws attention to the connection between the *fast* nature of the food and its consequences – *fatness*.

Or take the phrase 'traumatised by testing'. Without the alliteration, 'testing' could be seen as a quite neutral word, but linked by sound to 'traumatised' it makes the experience sound quite terrifying.

Sometimes the clue is in the sound itself. Words such as 'dead', 'doomed' and 'dreaded' contain the drumbeat of a heavy dull sound, which adds to the emotional strength of the phrase. On the other hand, 'lighter' sounds such as 'f', 't' and 'l' can express a more frivolous mood, e.g. 'flutter', 'flighty', 'trilling'.

Repetition of words

Example

> *Too much stuff. Endless piles of stuff.*

The repetition of the word 'stuff' emphasises the sheer amount of things and the word choice of 'stuff' suggests in the first place that the things are not particularly valuable or well-chosen – the overall impression is of a pile of useless rubbish.

Repetition of phrases

Example

> *It is a sight at once heartening and shaming. Heartening because it is good to see that people are still willing to give up time, money and effort to care with great sensitivity and respect for those they have never met. Shaming because, in global terms, 'we are a wealthy country', and in a wealthy country people should not go hungry.*

? Question

- How is the phrase 'heartening and shaming' given more force by repetition? (**Answer (20)** on page 87.)

Repetition of structures

Example

> *The worst thing about poverty is a sense of shame. The worst thing about joblessness is a sense of personal dishonour. The sense that you are just a mote in a great pool of floating labour, deprived of choice, will never go away.*

The repetition of the two short sentences, each beginning 'The worst thing about …', makes sure that the reader is focused on just how bad the situation is.

The rule of three

The 'rule of three' or 'triad' describes how using words, phrases, clauses or sentences in groups of three adds power to the ideas. It doesn't really matter what you call this feature of language as long as you explain its effect. There is something very powerful in the use of three terms to catch the attention, to hold interest and to make something memorable.

Hints & tips ★

A number of the questions throughout the Analysis section of this book are much narrower and more specific than the questions you may get in the exam. In a typical exam question, you might be asked specifically about word choice or imagery, etc.; but it is equally likely that the question would ask 'by referring to at least two features of language …'. It is on these occasions that you have to remind yourself of the features of language discussed here.

Famous people throughout the ages have understood and used this:

Julius Caesar:

> *I came. I saw. I conquered.*

This suggests a tremendous sense of power.

Winston Churchill:

> *I have, myself, full confidence that if all do their duty, if nothing is neglected, and if the best arrangements are made, as they are being made, we shall prove ourselves once more able to defend our island home, to ride out the storm of war, and to outlive the menace of tyranny, if necessary for years, if necessary alone.*

Here Churchill uses the trick twice: 'if all …'; 'if nothing …'; 'and if the best …' and, in the second half of the sentence, 'to defend our island home'; 'to ride out the storm'; 'to outlive the menace'.

Barack Obama:

> *If there is anyone out there who still doubts that America is a place where all things are possible; who still wonders if the dream of our founders is alive in our time; who still questions the power of our democracy – tonight is your answer.*

This example is from one of the articles on food banks.

Example

> *It has become normal with astonishing speed. Wages are depressed while bills rise ever upward. Pensions and savings descend to the level of a lottery. Education, once the route to security, has left us with legions of well-read casual labourers. For those not granted even that promise there is the zero hours contract, the bedroom tax, the abolition of any right to social security, and the stigma of poverty.*

> *The last of these is nothing new. The poor were always marked out. Now we find elaborate ways to describe the old facts: fuel poverty, food poverty, 'poverty of aspiration'.*

? Question

- Identify two examples where a sequence of three items has been used to create an effect. (**Answer (21)** on page 87.)

Tone

As its name suggests, tone is initially a description of a sound. The tone of a piece of writing becomes obvious when it is read out loud by someone who understands what is going on. You would be in a much better place in the exam if the passages were read out to you in the correct tone – but that is not about to happen!

Hidden tones

It is especially important to catch the tone if the writer is using an ironic, playful, mocking or humorous tone. Unfortunately, if you don't recognise that you are in some way being played with, you could end up misunderstanding what is actually being said.

There is a particularly good example of this trap in one of the passages we looked at on page 49 about the technophobe who didn't use his mobile phone.

Example 1

> *I do have a mobile phone, but it's immobile. I never take it out of the house, for fear of triggering some ridiculous trend in which a horde of people march down the street bawling into these sinister little gadgets. If you allowed people to use mobile phones in public, you might end up being forced to listen to them on trains and in cafés, asking noisily whether the invoices have arrived. The prospect is too appalling to contemplate.*
>
> *…*
>
> *Nowadays however, protest is most definitely what my email virginity has become. I am living proof that all this frenetic, mostly vacuous, communication is quite superfluous. We all survived without it before it started, and I personally have survived without it ever since. If people really want to contact me they write. If they can't be bothered, or have forgotten how to do it, that's their problem.*

The first paragraph only makes sense if you realise that the writer is mocking the actuality of people doing exactly what he is describing, by pretending that it hasn't happened yet and suggesting how appalling it would be if such a situation were to come true. All the words like 'ridiculous', 'horde', 'bawling' and 'sinister' lead up to the idea of 'appalling', but the real clue is in 'If you allowed people to use mobile phones in public' – obviously he knows, and he knows that we know, that this situation already exists, but he is pretending that it doesn't and that the world would be a better place without this phenomenon.

Example 2

> *[The sport minister] had recently watched girls aged 7–17 doing inline skating at a YMCA event and said: 'Those girls … looked absolutely gorgeous. They were wearing their socks pulled up – beautiful socks with sequins – and their hair was done; my goodness they could skate.'*
>
> *Beautiful socks; 'done' hair. I'm swooning as I type, especially on behalf of the seven-year-olds judged on their looks. Never mind, say, Nicola Adams and her gold in boxing at the London*

Olympics – where were her sequined socks? Or Gemma Gibbons with her untidy hair and her silver medal in judo. Or Jessica Ennis running about in a really fast and unfeminine manner doing heptathlons.

(?) Question

- What is the tone of the second paragraph here, and what words or expressions give you evidence for your opinion? (**Answer (22)** on page 88.)

Example 3

They do watch a lot of telly. They spend a fair dollop of time on the computer: sometimes they're genuinely doing their homework! They eat chips. They like chicken nuggets, and burgers. They eat sweets. And what's more, in yet another example of the so-called poison culture in which experts tell us our kids are now being raised, my husband and I spend a fair bit of time actually hoping they'll do well. When they do a test or an exam, we like them to pass it. If they don't come up to scratch we make sure we tell them that they're not doing well enough: you can do better, so do better!

So, presumably, we are nightmare parents, raising a nightmare generation on a poisonous cocktail of junk food, marketing, over-competitive schooling and electronic entertainment.

Hints & tips

A number of the questions throughout the Analysis section of this book are much narrower and more specific than the questions you may get in the exam. In a typical exam question, you might be asked specifically about word choice or imagery, etc.; but it is equally likely that the question would ask 'by referring to at least two features of language…' It is on these occasions that you have to remind yourself of the features of language discussed here.

(?) Question

- What is the overall tone of these two paragraphs?

Answer

- Obviously the parents don't actually think they are 'nightmare parents' – probably the opposite, so you could say that the tone is sarcastic, and that would show that you have recognised that these sentences are not to be taken literally.
- A better description of the tone might be 'sceptical'. The use of 'so-called', 'experts' and 'presumably' cast doubt or scorn on the opinion of the experts about how to bring up children. They, as parents, don't believe the experts.

Straightforward tones

Other tones are easier: anger, indignation, curiosity, nostalgia, enthusiasm, and so on.

Example 1

When I do get ground down, when it feels really relentless, I have to be reminded that this is not for ever and that I'm travelling emotionally, if not geographically. I'm learning about myself, developing the patience and sympathy that I never even thought I lacked. Best of all, Jack and I like each other. I'm always pleased to see him. We spend nearly every waking hour together, yet when I'm not with him I miss him. I know what 'poi' and 'sha' mean. Above all, I know in every bone of my body that I will never regret this. I will not lie on my deathbed and think, oh, how I wish I'd spent less time with my son.

? Question

- The tone is probably best described as sincere, enthusiastic or emotional. Consider how you would be able to back up any one of these descriptions by using evidence from the paragraph. (**Answer (23)** on page 88.)

Example 2

DIVIDED WE FALL

The poor suffer, the politicians spin ... Britain becomes a cruel and nasty place

? Question

- Show how this headline and subheading suggest the tone of the article and the writer's stance on the issue. (**Answer (24)** on page 88.)

Example 3

Who truly believes that someone applies to a food bank for fun or a scam? Who exists a wage slip away from the same oblivion yet still mutters that folk should be grateful for exploitation wages?

? Question

- Identify an appropriate tone in these lines and explain how the evidence supports your choice of tone. (**Answer (25)** on page 88.)

Evaluation of longer extracts and passages

This section is designed to help with two kinds of questions that are typically asked in an exercise dealing with two linked passages – the kind of passages you will face in the exam.

We have had a quick look at some of them earlier in the book, but we need to focus on them a little more closely now because this section is all about **the passage as a whole**.

The two typical questions might be:

- **Evaluate the effectiveness of a paragraph** [or possibly of a sentence] **as a conclusion to the whole passage** [or possibly to a substantial portion of the passage].
- **Identify key areas on which the two passages agree or disagree** [or possibly agree and disagree].

There are three important skills to help with these questions.
1 identifying the writer's stance or point of view
2 summarising
3 comparing.

Identifying the writer's stance

The writer's stance can be hinted at by **tone**. It also becomes obvious in the course of the article through the **argument** of the passage and the **use of language**. You will notice that many of the examples we have looked at under different language features have been aimed at showing what the writer's **attitude** is to his or her material.

If you read carefully, you should be able to tell what the writer's stance is and to provide evidence to demonstrate why you think so.

Tone

Example 1

All kids want for Christmas is technology

But will those gifts do them more harm than good?

Like many parents, I have been stewing over whether to give the gift of technology to my sons aged six and four. They, of course, like many kids, want their own screens. So why am I reluctant (financial cost aside) to give them what they want?

(?) Question

- What tone can you identify in this opening to an article on children's use of new media? How does it allow you to infer what the writer's stance is likely to be?

Answer

- The tone is possibly puzzled or ambivalent (remember this word from way back on page 37).
- The writer's stance, therefore, is likely to move from one side of the argument to the other, possibly not reaching any firm decision.

If you wanted to justify your choice of tone you could use the following ideas:

- The use of 'but' shows a contradiction; 'stewing' suggests an inability to decide; the use of self-questioning – 'So why am I … ?'
- The use of an informal register ('kids', 'stewing') and the parenthesis in the last line suggests that the answer will not be an official, expert, formal one.

Example 2

I am not connected

I shall soon be the only EMV (email virgin) left in the country. I have never sent an email, though I've occasionally cheated and asked my teenage son to do so for me. Nor have I ever used the internet. I am no more capable of going online than I am of getting to Saturn. I don't know how to text. I do have a mobile phone, but it's immobile.

Both the headline and the content of this opening show that the tone is light-hearted and mocking, and that the writer's stance is eccentric, deliberately setting his face against modern technology. If you know the term 'Luddite', now would be the time to use it.

Remember

It is really important to check out the tone of the passage and be alert to the fact that there might be irony at work (sometimes coupled with exaggeration) – in which case not all statements can be taken at face value.

Argument

The writer's argument will identify which side the writer is on or it might show that the writer is balanced on the subject and comes down on neither side.

Use of language

All the work in the Analysis section of this chapter helped to identify the writer's stance by taking into account such features as **word choice**, **imagery** and **structure**.

Summarising

This skill of summarising is important in many spheres, not not just in the examination. There is a world out there which education is preparing you for. The exam is merely a staging post on the way, not an end in itself – although it may be hard for you to see that as you come closer to taking the exam. In business, ideas have to be summarised, meetings have to be minuted; in any management role, ideas and instructions coming from above in the organisation's structure have to be transmitted in an easily accessible form to the people who will execute them; in medical or legal situations there have to be digests or summaries of consultations; your school reference is a summary of your talents and interests.

In the context of the passages used in the exam, summarising efficiently will help you to understand the whole of the article, or a section of it, rather than merely the little bits you have looked at in the questions.

It is important to be able to summarise quite lengthy passages quickly. This does not mean that you have to write an elegant, short version of what is in front of you. In fact, you don't have to write anything at all. Highlighting might be enough. For our purposes, summarising means being able to notice the important points in the argument of the passage(s) which, eventually, you are going to have to compare. We have already looked at part of this skill on page 33 in Reading paragraphs to **identify argument** and again when discussing **links** on pages 41–45.

The clue to successful summarising lies in understanding how paragraph structure works. You need to be able to:
- identify the topic sentence of a paragraph
- identify any really important development of the topic within the paragraph
- ignore unnecessary detail – examples, lists, descriptions, etc.

Look at the article below, which is about food banks. **Topic sentences** have been underlined for you. **Important developments/ideas** have been highlighted in bold. **Unnecessary detail** includes:
- lines 25–31 – 'The pity … on his own' is an example, not necessary in a summary
- lines 41–49 – 'I spoke to … into care' are again examples.

Example 1

Food banks or dignity: is that the choice we offer the hungry?

The rise of food banks in Britain has been met with shock, and denial. But they cannot cope with a national crisis

When people used to speak of hunger – as an issue, not a sensation – they used to speak of faraway. Hunger meant the developing world, NGOs, imploring eyes on the TV news. It was, in modern times at least, a distant problem. <u>So it comes as a
5   *shock that in the second decade of the twenty-first century we are speaking about hunger in Britain, right here right now.</u>*

Perhaps we were reassured by the notion that we live in the age of 'relative poverty', when those who were officially deemed poor were not actually destitute but just had less than everyone

10 _else._ The poor of our era were, we imagined, not Charles Dickens poor. They still had food on the table and a roof over their heads. Perhaps that is why there has been something of a delayed reaction to the rise and rise of genuine hunger in this country. The unkind would call it denial. **But it is becoming**

15 **harder to deny.**

Especially when I visited a Trussell Trust foodbank this week, in Hackney in East London, no more than a three-minute walk from a pleasant green complete with upmarket cafés and a specialist Italian deli. **It is a sight at once heartening and**

20 **shaming.** Heartening because it is good to see that people are still willing to give up time, money and effort to care with great sensitivity and respect for those they have never met. _Shaming because, in global terms, 'we are a wealthy country', and in a wealthy country people should not go hungry._

25 The pity of it is inescapable. I saw a man take home a couple of carrier bags filled with the most basic kind of basics: tinned sausages, a can of soup, a packet of pasta. All decent enough, each allocation calculated for balance by nutritionists. Except that you and I would not want to live on that for three days, which is

30 how long it has to last. And the Trussell rules say that he can only get such help twice more. After that, he will be on his own.

Should we be happy that neighbours, not some faceless state bureaucracy, are helping the hungry? Nice in theory, until you see the extreme pressure food banks are under, the days

35 they run out of food, the fact that affluent areas often, and predictably, get more donations than the poor areas that need most. **That's the trouble with a voluntary system,** designed to give emergency help only: it cannot cope with what is a nationwide crisis.

40   <u>*This view of a benign society also fails to reckon with shame.*</u>
I spoke to a Glasgow volunteer who told me she knows of men
too proud to use their local food bank, who instead walk miles
out of their way so they can get food for their families without
being seen by their neighbours. They cannot afford the bus, and

45   *the walk home carrying bags of tins is hard, but it preserves at*
least some dignity. I learned too of the single mothers who fear
visiting a food bank, thereby admitting they cannot feed their
children, lest they be deemed incapable and their kids taken
into care.

50   <u>*This was why Britons sought to put the Victorian era of charity*</u>
<u>*behind us, why we decided that sometimes a state service is*</u>
<u>*better:*</u> *because there is less shame in claiming a nationally*
authorised benefit than in going to a church hall, being handed
a food parcel and having to nod your head and say thank you.

55   <u>*Still, the shame is bearable if the alternative is you or your*</u>
<u>*family going hungry. What has become of us, when that is the*</u>
<u>*choice we offer our fellow citizens: dignity or food? And this in*</u>
<u>*our wealthy, wealthy country.*</u>

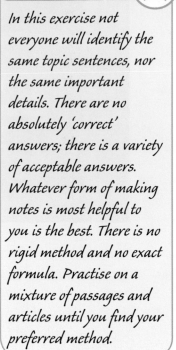

Hints & tips

In this exercise not everyone will identify the same topic sentences, nor the same important details. There are no absolutely 'correct' answers; there is a variety of acceptable answers. Whatever form of making notes is most helpful to you is the best. There is no rigid method and no exact formula. Practise on a mixture of passages and articles until you find your preferred method.

? Question

- Using the help provided, make some notes to identify the main points/ argument of the passage. (**Answer (26)** on page 88.)

The next example is shorter, but it will give you practice in making your own notes on the important ideas. You have seen various parts of this article before, so you have some knowledge of it.

Example 2

All kids want for Christmas is technology

But will those gifts do them more harm than good?

Like many parents, I have been stewing over whether to give the gift of technology to my sons aged six and four. They, of course, like many kids, want their own screens. So why am I reluctant (financial cost aside) to give them what they want?

5   *The American Academy of Pediatrics advises that children have less than two hours of screen time a day – and no digital media for the under twos. Yet a survey published last week showed that in the UK around half of two- to three-year-olds – dubbed 'iTods' – are playing on tablets.*

10 *So great is the urge to restrict this aspect of children's lives that there are even apps that will switch the machine off when the allotted time is up. Many tech advocates encourage such limits as part of the general boundary-making of parenting.*

15 *Scientific research on the subject is in its infancy and existing research is contradictory. If you believe that 'screen time' is bad for children, you can find a few pieces of research to support that view, which shows correlations with attention defici or with obesity. But there is other research that*
20 *suggests possible benefits: correlations, for instance, between computer skills and better IQs.*

Similarly, where some studies suggest that technology is making us more isolated, there are others that show the opposite. One study found that Facebook users had more
25 *social capital than abstainers, and that the site increased feelings of wellbeing especially in those suffering from low self-esteem.*

And there is a whole tranche of research claiming that technology can be good for children, especially when used in
30 *interaction with real-life scenarios in groups or with parents engaging in play too. This is not technology as babysitter, but as part of the general hard work of coaching and educating. Frankly it sounds a bit of a slog. However, the conclusion appears to be that we should be more relaxed about letting*
35 *children explore technology on their own. The world is changing: we are living in a world of social media and instant access to information. We cannot – and should not – turn the clock back. The problematic aspects of new technologies are also what is really positive about these technologies.*

For a sample summary see **Answer (27)** on page 88.

Hints & tips

How you make notes is entirely up to you. No one is going to look at them. They are simply a means to an end – finding the important ideas. You can highlight or even just remember – whatever suits you best.

Summary 👍

1 Identify topic sentences.
2 Identify the main supporting ideas.
3 Cut unnecessary detail.

Comparing

This skill of comparing is necessary to tackle the last question in the exam – the one where you have to compare two passages.

You will be asked to **identify key** areas on which the writers of the passages **agree** or **disagree** (or possibly, depending on the nature of the passages, where they agree **and** where they disagree). You will also be asked to '**refer in detail** to **both** passages'.

1   Look at the headings of both passages. There will be some information there – a general outline or simply an identification of the topic.
2   Look at the question(s) that ask you to compare the two passages – there will be some clues there as to what you are looking for overall.
3   Read both passages quickly.

Avoid the temptation to get stuck into the questions on the first passage without quickly reading the second one. If you don't read the second one now, you will have no idea where you are ultimately going with the ideas. You will see individual details, but not how these details contribute to the big picture.

When you have read both passages quickly, you can then get down to looking at the questions on Passage 1. Some part of your mind might be worrying away at the second passage even though you are giving your full conscious attention to Passage 1. (This way of working can apply to the Critical Reading paper as well – see Chapter 5.)

When you have finished answering the detailed questions, you should have some idea of the main points and what the writer's stance is.

If there is a question about the conclusion of the first passage, or part of it, it might help to give an overview of the important ideas.

Although you may not be asked individual questions on the second passage, you will have to be clear about its main ideas. There is the suggestion at the top of the second passage that 'you may wish' to make notes or to highlight main ideas. Obviously, it is in your own interests to take 'you may wish' and replace it with 'you should' or 'you must'! In the previous section on summarising you have practised doing exactly that. But because you know what you are looking for – agreement – for example, you can possibly skip quite quickly over some areas of Passage 2.

The second part of the question – '**refer in detail** to **both** passages' – means that you have to provide evidence by comment and reference to both passages to substantiate or back up your identification of a key point on which the writers agree (or disagree). So, for each key idea you have to show how that key point is made in **each** passage.

Hints & tips

When you are deciding on which areas are 'key', you have to be selective. There could, in a long passage, be quite a number of agreements, but you are looking to select the most important ones – probably three or four.

Hints & tips ⭐

You must do what you are asked. If you are asked about 'agree', then you ignore any areas of disagreement; if you are asked about 'disagree', then you ignore any areas of agreement. When you are asked to do both, of course, you do both. You must ignore what your feelings and ideas are on the subject. You are asked to make an objective identification of the main areas of agreement etc., so your views are irrelevant.

The next exercise consists of two passages for comparison:

'I am not connected' (page 49)

'All kids want for Christmas is technology' (pages 76–77)

Read the two passages and answer the question below.

? Question

- Both writers express their views about modern advances in communication technology. Identify **one** key area on which they disagree. In your answer you should refer in detail to both passages.

Note: the passages are both much shorter than you would come across in the exam and you have already seen both of them at various points throughout this book.

The value of doing this exercise is not so much in the actual answer, which is very easy, but in the methodology and explanation that follows the answer. Because they are so short, the question only asks for **one** key area of disagreement.

Answer

- The key area of disagreement is whether modern advances in communication technology are good for society or bad.
- The first passage is completely anti-technology/technophobic/ Luddite. He regards all of them as intrusive ('The prospect is too appalling to contemplate') and unnecessary – instead of 'frenetic, mostly vacuous communication', this can be done in old-fashioned writing.
- The second passage, on the whole, comes to the conclusion that modern advances are good for society. For example, 'Facebook users had more social capital than abstainers' as they increase general happiness and confidence; these means of communication are a valuable part of the world we live in – 'We cannot, and should not, turn the clock back'.

This answer has identified one key area of disagreement and has referred to each of the passages (not all references have to be quotations) to show what each writer's stance is.

Hints & tips

- *The answer does not refer to parts of the first four paragraphs of the second passage where the writer does have some doubts about the value of the technology, because that would be exploring an area of agreement, which is not what you were asked to do.*
- *The answer also does not make any reference to the car accident – that is merely supporting detail, not the key idea.*

The next exercise consists of two passages for comparison, 'To bring girls into sport, get rid of old ideas of femininity' and 'Oh do try to be more feminine, you sporting goddesses'.

Passage 1

To bring girls into sport, get rid of old ideas of femininity

It happened overnight. One minute, I was flying down the wing like a character out of *Bunty*, my only worry in life that I would lose control of the ball and thus let down our captain Caroline 'Caz' Johnson, a girl who seriously demanded to be impressed.
5   The next, I was a *Jackie* photo-strip, obsessed with frosted lipstick and whether my hair looked like Siobhan's out of *Bananarama*.

After this, there was no way back. Reluctant to run or indeed make sudden movements of any kind, I was soon dropped from the hockey team. PE lessons, meanwhile, became a convoluted
10   exercise in avoidance – and not only for me. The slothfulness spread among us girls like a contagion. Cross-country runs began with a truculent jog until we were out of sight of the teachers, at which point we would repair to the nearest newsagent for sweets and a Coke. Rounders involved making sure your team was out as
15   soon as possible, the better that you might field, and get to sun-bathe and gossip in the long grass. Athletics meant hiding in the loos until it was 'too late to change, Miss'.

Needless to say, I never returned to sport, for all that I secretly longed to. At university, I did not row or take up cricket. My 20s
20   were notable for the amount of time I spent sleeping. These days, I run twice a week, but I do it only for my waistline: it's work, and it's lonely work at that.

When my husband comes home from his weekly football game, I am full of envy. The boyish pleasure it gives him! The camaraderie!

25   So when the sports minister said that she worries some women find sport 'unfeminine', I am prepared – unlike some – to give her the benefit of the doubt. Trying for empathy, she missed her $\Rightarrow$

⇨ footing and ended up sounding only patronising. But, her solution to the question of why so many women disdain sport – 1.8 million

30 fewer women than men take part in it regularly – certainly sounds loathsome to me (she considers cheerleading and rollerskating to be 'very feminine' and thinks those who take part in them look, as if they were starring in ads for antiperspirant, 'absolutely radiant').

But this doesn't mean that she's wrong about the problem itself. It's

35 the idea of 'femininity' that needs a rethink, not sport. Better still, we could ditch the word altogether. Meanwhile, we need to stop thinking of certain other words – 'ambition', 'success', even 'clever' all come to mind – as dirty when placed in proximity to the name of a woman. What's wrong with wanting to win, with longing to be

40 good at something? And the lead must come from the top.

Women who have succeeded need to start talking about what they feel in their guts, however painful they may find this, whatever damage it may do to the air of diffidence they've spent so many years carefully cultivating.

45 They need to transmit their excitement, their satisfaction, their sense of liberation and empowerment.

When I think back to the *Bananarama* days, my hair crisp with Sun-In and Wella gel, it is this flimsiness that pains me most, the sense that I would only be noticed, be found attractive, if I was a

50 blonde smile in stretch jeans. I can't deny that in my nylon hockey skirt and clumpy studded boots, my knees covered in mud and my sweaty fringe in my eyes, I felt that I looked too substantial, too challenging. And that feeling stayed with me for years, long after my hockey stick had been laid to rest in the attic.

55 How I wish I'd known then what I know now, which is that energy, zest and, above all, strength are twice as attractive as a pampered skin and at least three times as enduring.

Passage 2

Oh do try to be more feminine, you sporting goddesses

Last Thursday the minister for sport suggested that women who play sport don't have to feel unfeminine, that sports such as ballet, gymnastics, cheerleading and even roller-skating, which can be performed at a high level, can leave those participating looking

5 radiant and very feminine.

She had recently watched girls aged 7–17 doing inline skating at a YMCA event and said: 'Those girls … looked absolutely gorgeous. They were wearing their socks pulled up – beautiful socks with sequins – and their hair was done; my goodness they could skate.'

10 Beautiful socks; 'done' hair. I'm swooning as I type, especially on behalf of the seven-year-olds judged on their looks. Never mind, ⇨

⇨ say, Nicola Adams and her gold in boxing at the London Olympics – where were her sequined socks? Or Gemma Gibbons with her untidy hair and her silver medal in judo. Or Jessica Ennis running
15 about in a really fast and unfeminine manner doing heptathlons.

Imagine being minister for sport and equalities and thinking that ballet and cheerleading (not actually a sport) are good for the body image of young women.

Cheerleading looks very jolly (I'll give it that much), especially
20 if you spent your formative years watching films and television programmes set in American high schools, most of which make a point of clearly demarcating the pretty and popular cheerleaders from the tragic 'loser' girls who have brains.

Before I wear out my keyboard with dismantling the minister's
25 unfortunate remarks, I should point out that buried inside them is a micro-kernel of truth. At the age of 14 boys don't long to ask you out because you are freakishly strong or because you came to their rescue in a fight, like a roaring teenage she-Hulk.

However, the fact that teenage boys can be intimidated by sporty
30 girls – just as middle-aged men can be cowed by powerful female bosses – is obviously not an ideal state of affairs.

The remedy for such teenage boys does not consist of shunting the problem into sequin-socked sidings. No, the one thing that can gnaw at the dated idea that the only appropriate exercise for girly
35 girls is twerking is the precise opposite – that more girls should do 'proper' sports, and do them free of people labelling them or complaining they lack radiance.

The unfeminine sports are the solution, not the problem.

? Question

- Both writers express their views about girls' sport and femininity. Identify two key areas on which they agree. In your answer you should refer in detail to both passages. (**Answer (28)** on page 89.)

Hints & tips ⭐

- *Some parts of each passage may have nothing to do with the key areas, so you can ignore them.*
- *The tone of each writer is important in showing the writer's stance – especially if that tone has elements of irony, sarcasm or humour.*
- *The evidence in support of each of the key areas should be a mixture of quotation/reference and comment. It is not enough just to give a quotation – you have to make a link with your key area.*
- *If you are not asked for a specific number of key areas, you should probably be looking for no more than three or four.*

Summary

1 What **topic** – or **aspect** of the topic – in the passages are you being asked about?
2 Are you being asked about **agreement** or **disagreement** or **both**?
3 **Identify** the **key** areas of agreement or disagreement or both.
4 By referring to **both** passages, provide backing for **each** area you have identified.

Hints & tips

1 *Don't make any reference to your own feelings and attitudes towards the topic.*
2 *Do check whether the whole topic is to be explored, or an aspect of the topic.*
3 *Don't identify too many areas of agreement/disagreement — distinguish between the important and the trivial.*
4 *Don't stray into areas of disagreement if what you have been asked involves areas of agreement — and vice versa.*

Answers

There are three important points to make about the answers.

1 These are possible answers – not the only answers.
2 There are many more points contained in these answers than you would need to produce for a given question. Look at the mark allocation and use it as a guide to how many points you will have to make.
3 The **commentaries on the answers** are even more important than the answers themselves because they show the method of arriving at a good answer.

Note: it is not always repeated in every answer but:
1 A reference alone gains no marks. A basic comment is worth 1 mark, whereas a detailed, insightful comment can be worth 2 marks.
2 You must use your own words as far as possible: you should make clear you know the meaning of complex words; simple words can obviously be repeated without trying to find a synonym.

Answers

Answer (1) (page 39)

1 The large number and great variety of new forms of communication.

The context of 'proliferation of technology' – the list of items that children now have – helps you to arrive at your answer.

2 The fact that children may be able to outwit their parents or conceal things from them.

The context of 'the challenge to adult authority' – they are more competent than their parents – helps to give you your answer.

Answer (2) (page 40)

1 Participating in clubs sharing your enthusiasms.
2 Volunteering to help in the community.
3 Experiencing the world of business start-ups.

Again, punctuation helps with this answer. There are four sentences in the section of the paragraph you need to use. The last sentence simply gives more details of the charity shop idea. Thus each of the remaining three sentences gives you one point to identify. If you had produced a list of clubs you would be getting tied up in the detail and not seeing the bigger picture in the whole paragraph. You must focus on the 'topics' not the details.

Answer (3) (page 41)

Technology:
- teaches children facts and skills (educational)
- helps children make friends (social)
- helps develop children's imagination through computer games (educational).

Here you have two items in one sentence, and then a longer sentence that you have to work through to see that the main point is that of the development of the imagination. You have been asked about benefits, therefore the mention of violence is not part of your answer.

Answer (4) (page 42)

The rest of the paragraph offers three main solutions that might help 'employability'. Good exam passes are important, but so are marketable skills such as the ability to work in a variety of situations, creativity and good careers advice, including knowing your personal strengths, making useful choices and researching universities' requirements.

Or it would be acceptable to put your answer in this form:

The rest of the paragraph offers three main solutions that might help to get employment:

- not only good exam passes
- but marketable skills
- and good careers advice.

The development here is in the 'problem/solution' idea: these are solutions to the problem set out in the first sentence. It is then a simple matter to identify these three solutions.

Answer (5) (page 45)

- 'Those demands' are the result of so many people needing to eat fish so more fish needs to be caught, but sustainably.
- 'That', i.e. the need to catch fish sustainably, 'makes it all the more crucial' to stop illegal fishing – which is unsustainable.

Answer (6) (page 47)

The idea of 'the print revolution' and the idea that contradictory research always accompanies new technology are illustrated by the examples of telephone and radio, which are now uncontroversial, and even more spectacularly by the idea that reading novels was once thought to be dangerous for young people.

Answer (7) (page 47)

The anecdote shows that even when a mobile phone could have been legitimately useful (i.e. in an emergency situation), it failed to be of any use. This supports the author's general view – that mobile phones are unnecessary/useless.

Answer (8) (page 49)

- The conclusion refers back to the author's description of himself as an email virgin in the opening sentence of the passage.
- The words 'frenetic', with its connotations of lots of useless activity, 'vacuous', with its connotations of emptiness and futility, 'superfluous', with its suggestion of too much useless stuff, all refer to his description of people engaged in banal mobile phone communication.
- The fact that he is not engaged in these forms of communication goes back to the title.
- The last sentence emphasises his stance on the subject by putting all the blame on other people and by making the distinction between important communication and mere remarks, therefore justifying his views (at least to himself).

There is far more in this answer than you would actually be required to write, but it shows understanding of the way in which:

- *writing techniques aid the effectiveness of the ending*
- *the ideas of the passage are summed up.*

Answer (9) (page 52)

- 'sumptuously' suggests the luxury and excessive attractiveness of the fish.
- 'juicy' suggests moist and tasty.

- 'fizzing' suggests something energetic and full of potential.
- 'drizzle of virgin olive oil' suggests a thin stream of something precious added to the fish.
- 'virgin olive oil' suggests fresh, new, unpolluted accompaniment for the fish.
- 'splash' suggests the idea of a chef-like flourish adding to the taste.
- 'zingiest' suggests a fresh and tangy flavour being added to the dish.

Again, there are too many examples here; three would probably be sufficient, but it would depend on the number of marks available. The word 'suggests' is used in these answers to show that you are moving from the reference (for which you get no marks) to the connotative area surrounding the word you have chosen to deal with.

Answer (10) (page 53)

This paragraph does not have so many obvious examples to choose. There are really no words that stand out in the first four lines – all the words are pretty much used in their simple denotational sense.

But the last three lines provide some scope for an answer:
- 'mulling' suggests giving time to thinking over the contents in a leisurely way.
- 'surfing' – although 'surfing the web' is now seen as a simply denotational description of looking up stuff on the internet, 'surfing' still has the feeling of something joyous and exciting.
- 'popping out' suggests the ability to leave the house spontaneously, on a mere whim.
- 'pleasure shopping' suggests shopping not for necessities but for more interesting, must-have items.
- 'shop floor' suggests he is tied to the same place for work and living in a never-ending time loop.

'popping out' and 'pleasure shopping' are the most straightforward. 'mulling' would be good if you knew what it meant. You might not have thought of 'surfing' because you felt it was just (in this context) an 'ordinary' word. And 'shop floor' is a bit more complicated.

Answer (11) (page 54)

The simile 'The slothfulness spread among us girls like a contagion' suggests that slothfulness (laziness) was infectious and began to affect all the girls. Comparing the lack of action to a disease suggests that the writer now thinks this was a bad thing that happened to her and to all the other girls.

Answer (12) (page 55)

By comparing himself and the other househusbands to blue whales, which are solitary creatures who only rarely meet other blue whales but when they do they remain together for a while for companionship, the writer emphasises the fact that there are not very many men in his situation and when they find each other they stick together for mutual support.

Answer (13) (page 57)

'More honey than poison in the cocktail' is seeing life as a drink that the children will take, but the idea that twenty-first century childhood is somehow dangerous (poison) is being opposed by the idea that life is actually very pleasant for these children – as sweet as honey.
Life for the modern child is made up of good things and bad – this is the literal idea; figuratively, life is seen as a mixed drink (a cocktail) containing good things (honey) and bad things (poison) but with more good than bad.

Answer (14) (page 58)

In this metaphor childhood is seen as a country that is the subject of a dispute, as if people don't know the boundaries of the country, and the geography of the country is like the knowledge of how it feels to be a child in that landscape.

The metaphor is extended when the country of childhood is forgotten by adults and replaced with their version of the landscape (universe).
You don't need to deal with the extension if you are happy with your answer on the 'territory/geography' idea.

Answer (15) (page 58)

'Plundering shoals' is the obvious metaphor. It suggests that when ordinary people buy fish in a supermarket, they are acting like thieves or pirates in 'stealing' from the world's stock of fish, and the stock in the supermarket is described as a 'shoal' because so many of the fish are being sold. This gives the impression that consumption of fish is so great that something needs to be done.

'Zombies' and 'slicing the kitchen knife through the cast of Finding Nemo' *are both possibilities, but much harder to comment on. And there is also a simile: 'shriek like seagulls'.*
You would only be expected to deal with one or two of these. As a guide, look at the number of marks on offer.

Answer (16) (page 58)

The metaphor 'savage' suggests that the fishing system is out of control and violently tearing into the large fish species, just as a predator would savage another animal.

This answer deals with 'savage' as a metaphor; it could also be dealt with as personification. The first part of the answer, up to 'species', would make a perfectly acceptable comment on the word choice of 'savage' because it deals with the connotations of savage in this context.

Answer (17) (page 59)

This use of imagery is effective because it suggests that the 'blonde smile' has reduced the girl to a mere aspect of her appearance – ignoring things like the quality of her mind and other worthwhile attributes – which, along with the 'stretch jeans', suggests that she is only interested in her appearance and what effect it will have on others.

Answer (18) (page 60)

'Spawned' and 'muscled' are usually used to describe the actions of human beings. Here 'gastroculture', which is an abstract, is seen to be powerful in creating large numbers of live events and in forcing its way into other larger events which up until now had no need of its services. The words are critical of gastroculture because 'spawned' suggests large quantities of offspring indiscriminately spreading around, and 'muscled' suggests the use of physical force to get where it wants to be.

Answer (19) (page 63)

- The semi-colon in the first line defines the two balancing but opposing strands of the argument.
- The list of positive qualities the writer finds in young people – 'imaginative, tenacious, versatile and well-grounded' – suggests that they are well equipped in all areas of personality.
- The short declarative sentence 'If … optimistic' ends the paragraph with a positive climax to the argument.

Answer (20) (page 67)

Each of the two aspects that the writer sees in the food banks is given weight by being repeated at the beginning of each of the next two sentences, each offering an explanation of what he means by 'heartening and shaming'.

Answer (21) (page 68)

- 'Wages', 'Pensions' and 'Education' begin three successive sentences, each of which presents a pessimistic view of the situation.
- 'fuel poverty', 'food poverty', 'poverty of aspiration' all help to expand the 'stigma of poverty' in the previous paragraph.

Answer (22) (page 70)

The writer is being sarcastic: she is not 'swooning' in admiration – she regards the comments about 'Beautiful socks' and 'done' hair as totally out of place when talking about sports. The questions are mocking the 'sequined' image, which has nothing to do with real female athletes.

Answer (23) (page 71)

- sincere – 'in every bone of my body'; 'I will never regret this'; 'on my deathbed'
- enthusiastic – 'Best of all'; 'always pleased to see him'; 'nearly every waking hour together'; plus some of the ones already mentioned.
- emotional – 'travelling emotionally'; 'developing the patience and sympathy'; 'Jack and I like each other'; 'I miss him'; plus some of the ones already mentioned.

Answer (24) (page 71)

- The tone of the article will be serious and probably angry. The words 'suffer' and 'cruel and nasty' are strong negative words that the writer is probably going on to justify.
- The writer's stance is likely to be on the side of the poor and against the politicians.

Answer (25) (page 71)

Tone: angry or indignant.

Quote: the use of questions; 'for fun or a scam'; 'oblivion'; 'exploitation wages'.

Comment:

- The questions have an implied answer, 'No one', which suggests that any right-minded person will agree with the writer's indignation.
- The juxtaposition of 'food bank' with 'fun' and 'scam' suggest that nobody wants to be connected with a food bank.
- 'Oblivion' and 'exploitation' are strongly negative words suggesting that the system is all wrong.

Because you have been asked to 'explain', a simple quotation, while necessary, is not enough. The quotation needs to be connected to a reasonable comment.

You would not use all of these answers. One, well explained, would be enough.

Answer (26) (page 76)

- it is shocking that real hunger exists in twenty-first century Britain.
- poor used to mean deprived of luxuries but not actually hungry.
- but you now see real hunger in food banks.
- good in one way (showing charity)/bad in the other (causing shame).
- charity is fine so long as it works, but sometimes it doesn't.
- charity also causes shame.
- that is why the state took over from charities.
- but if the state no longer provides, food banks are better than nothing.
- but it shouldn't be happening in a wealthy country.

There are lots of different ways of arriving at the main points and noting them. You have to find what suits you.

Answer (27) (page 77)

- problem – is new tech good for kids? (lines 1–4).
- one side says harmful/needs control (lines 5–14).
- research contradictory (lines 15–21).
- isolation possible; but social skills too (lines 22–27).
- good when interactive (lines 28–31).
- conclusion should be relaxed/can't turn the clock back/on the whole positive (lines 35–39).

Answer (28) (page 82)

In this question you have been asked to look for two key areas.

One way of starting might be to write down the two key areas you have found.

a) They agree on deploring the minister for sport's view of feminine/unfeminine sports.

OR

They agree that women should be concentrating on qualities other than appearance.

b) They agree that the problem is not the opposition between feminine/unfeminine sports, but with the whole idea of femininity/unfemininity in society.

You could then accumulate the evidence from each of the passages to back up each of these key areas.

Another way is to take each key area in turn and give the relevant supporting evidence, as shown in the following sample answer. You should identify quite clearly where the first of your key areas ends and the next one begins.

a) They agree on deploring the minister for sport's view of feminine/unfeminine sports.

Passage 1 – cheerleading and rollerskating sound 'loathsome' and the writer is sarcastic about the concentration on 'looks absolutely radiant'.

Passage 2 – the concentration on the sequined socks and the 'done hair' are scorned for their pressure on looks and body image.

OR

They agree that women should be concentrating on qualities other than appearance.

Passage 1 – it is not just about sport: women need to embrace words like 'ambition' and 'success', which are thought of as masculine traits.

Passage 2 – the idea is not to stop doing 'unfeminine' sports, but to change people's views on women in general. Unfeminine sports are part of the answer to women's situation.

b) They agree that the problem is not the opposition between feminine/unfeminine sports, but with the whole idea of femininity/unfemininity in society.

Passage 1 – 'It's the idea of "femininity" that needs a rethink, not sport' – the writer thinks the word is unhelpful for enabling women to achieve their deserved position in society.

Passage 2 – the unfeminine sports are the solution, not the problem. The pursuit of real achievement in sport cultivates the strengths needed to take on the world, instead of being obsessed by outward 'attractiveness'.

- *The first four paragraphs of Passage 1 (lines 1–24) can be ignored because the whole issue that the passages have in common is their reaction to the sport minister's statement.*
- *The tone of each passage helps to show the writers' stance(s) – very scathing.*
- *The evidence given in support of each of the key areas is a mixture of quotation/reference and comment.*
- *It is not enough just to give a quotation – you have to make a link with your key area.*
- *The serious point they are making is that the division between feminine and unfeminine is artificial and unhelpful to women's position in society.*
- *There are two alternatives for the first key area – but whichever one you choose, the idea of body image/appearance has to be there.*

The following two passages focus on the nature of Twitter.

Passage 1

In this passage Ian Bell, writing in the *Sunday Herald*, puts forward his views on Twitter. Read the passage and attempt the questions that follow.

Hints & tips ★

It would be best not to try this Practice Paper until you are sure you have understood the advice on how to approach the questions.

Is Twitter dumbing us down?

As of this morning, there are 7.2 billion people on the planet.

If you believe every claim, 1.19 billion of them are on Facebook. That's either an awful lot of people wedded to the champion of social media, or an indication of the vastly greater number who can't be
5   bothered or manage without. Ubiquity still eludes the social media.

The best example of this is probably Twitter. Some of its users behave as though all the world is attempting to communicate in messages no longer than 140 characters. The truth can be expressed as pithily: Twitter has a very long way to go before all
10   those grandiose evangelical claims of an interconnected humanity come close to being a reality. As of October 2013, the service had 500 million users – but only 215 million of those were 'active'.

Once I swore I would never have anything to do with Twitter. The number of people capable of saying anything of interest in
15   140 characters struck me as vanishingly small (it is). The number who could resist self-promotion, nastiness, or pursuing politics without using the typographic equivalent of A SHRIEK didn't seem impressive (it isn't). The attractions appeared limited.

Tweeting publicly, you can soon find yourself reminded that
20   the number of people you would cross a street to avoid hasn't diminished since last you checked. When Caroline Criado-Perez was subjected to anonymous threats of rape and death last summer for campaigning to have Jane Austen's image on a banknote, the case against Twitter was pretty convincing. Why
25   volunteer to introduce yourself to scum?

You could make a case. You could say, first, that by avoiding the ugliness and the risks you let thugs win. You could say that the contest about free speech matters. You could argue, above all, that disdain for change is not going to halt change.

⇨

⇨

30 I gave in to Twitter for less elevated reasons: the herd was
    thundering through. In journalism and politics in Scotland in
    2014, a year with some significance, Twitter amounts to an
    important, if ramshackle, forum. In terms of discourse, it is more
    like the badlands of the Wild West than Periclean Athens, but as a
35 responsive, collective medium Twitter is as staggeringly fast as it
    is flawed.

    Witnessing the Clutha tragedy as it unfolded was a case in
    point. That night, journalists and others all over Glasgow and
    Scotland mounted an impromptu rolling news operation through
40 Twitter that was wondrous to behold. No important fact reached
    traditional outlets that had not already been sourced and tweeted.
    A great deal of rubbish and rumour went through the mill, as ever,
    but the self-organising nature of the thing meant that nonsense
    was soon weeded out. The story was gathered and told as though
45 by an ideal virtual newsroom.

    Twitter is fascinating, meanwhile, if you have any interest in
    the forms of the written word. A lot of the better tweets are
    shaped like a classic gag, with set-up and pay-off. A lot of the
    very worst, even by 'educated' types, simply prove a truism:
50 some people really can't string two sentences together. As for
    the character limit, I feel an odd nostalgia. If you ever had to
    write headlines within the unbreakable rules of hot-metal type,
    when fonts could not by tweaked with clever software, tweeting
    isn't so hard.

55 But Twitter, like most of the social media, like most forms of
    digitised communication, attracts all sorts even as it excludes
    billions. The numbers who think a pinnacle of technological
    achievement is just a grand excuse for vile and sneaky abuse is
    staggering – social media bring the witless and the worst flocking,
60 much as dank, cosy shadows attract cockroaches.

    And there is an unpalatable fact: clever technology doesn't make
    the stupid any less stupid. In fact, there are numerous claims that
    fast, frictionless social media are making things worse – witness
    the claim from 2008 that attention spans shortened from 12
65 minutes to 5 minutes in the space of a decade.

    Is that claim true, however? It might be explained by an
    impeccable theory (mine): tales of social media reducing attention
    spans can probably be explained by people failing to pay attention.

    Suddenly there was a lot of talk of 'brain plasticity', the loss of
70 the ability to contemplate, of the evaporation of real thinking in
    an accelerated, overloaded world. Again, however, the scientific
    evidence was thin. It is too early to tell.

    But then, what does anyone need to know? Twitter is utterly
    facile – how could it be otherwise? If all you know is what
75 Google passes off as the only truth, what can you ever know? If
    information is grazed and attention flits like a butterfly, knowledge
    is a glittering shadow.

Questions

1 By referring to at least two features of language in lines 1–12, analyse how the writer establishes his critical stance on the topic of social media. **(4)**

2 Re-read lines 13–18.
   a) What, according to the writer, is wrong with the Twitter users he identifies in these lines? **(2)**
   b) Analyse how the writer's use of language in these lines emphasises the negative impression of Twitter he is promoting to his readers. You should refer in your answer to such features as sentence structure, word choice and tone. **(4)**

3 Re-read lines 26–29.
   What three pieces of evidence does the writer provide which might 'make a case' for joining Twitter? **(3)**

4 Re-read lines 30–36.
   a) Identify two reasons for his decision finally to give in to Twitter. **(2)**
   b) Analyse how the writer expresses his conflicting feelings about the network he is joining. You should refer in your answer to such features as word choice, imagery, contrast … **(4)**

5 Consider the section of the passage which deals specifically with Twitter (lines 13–60).
   Evaluate the effectiveness of lines 55–60 as a conclusion to the writer's discussion of Twitter's advantages and disadvantages. **(2)**

6 Read lines 61–77.
   Explain the main points of the writer's argument in these lines. **(4)**

Passage 2

In this second passage Josh Constine writes on the website of an organisation called techcrunch.com in November 2013.

Read the passage and attempt the question that follows. While reading, you may wish to make notes on the main ideas and/or highlight key points in the passage.

You should use Twitter because it makes everyone as smart as anyone

Twitter's purpose is still widely misunderstood, and many people think they have no need for it. But it has great potential to enlighten us. Here's how:

We are a specialised species. Each of us lives a different life with
5   unique passions, intellectual pursuits and hobbies. We choose a path and along the way amass a distinct collection knowledge. But what if we could peek into each other's minds to gain insight from the roads we'll never travel? Well, we can. That's the magic of Twitter.

It's inherently flexible. Twitter is a skeleton its users bring to
10   life. Yes, we can share what we're having for breakfast or what we watch on TV. But at its best, Twitter is a tool for distilling understanding of the world into the most digestible format possible.

Imagine a scientist on the other side of the planet. They read
15   and research all day, spending time the rest of us don't have. Then they filter through all the noise and esoteric details, choosing the most important things they've learned. The scientist condenses these complex concepts into simple, widely comprehensible 140-character slices of information, and tweets
20   them. Knowledge.

By following the right people on Twitter, we could see the world like a quantum physicist, movie critic, artist, explorer or entrepreneur. Even 'normal' people have something special to say about how they interpret existence, and there is joy in more
25   vividly seeing our friends' perspectives.

Reading tweets won't make us experts in all these areas. But our mortal lives are short. There's not enough time to grasp the intricacies of everything. Twitter is a shortcut to the next best alternative – understanding through the help of those who truly
30   understand.

But we do need to learn to follow the right people . . . and unfollow the wrong people. Twitter's uncensored stream of information is vulnerable to blatherers more interested in self-promotion and hearing themselves talk than educating their
35   audience. If these challenges can't be beaten, the value of Twitter falls apart.

While humankind has long sought to pool its knowledge, never has the process been so efficient, portable and accessible. We don't have to buy, lug around, and read through hundreds of
40   pages of a book to learn. We needn't lock ourselves in a library or laboratory. And we don't need personal friendships or private meetings with people to hear their thoughts. In fact, Twitter opens a two-way street between us all, ideally creating a conversation, not a broadcast.   ⇨

45 The internet gave everyone a way to share. But Twitter's character limit and real-time nature delivers us condensed, pre-filtered, ready-to-consume intelligence rather than making us hunt for it.

Twitter could spawn communities where there were once just scattered aficionados who thought they were alone. Its
50 distribution of information could empower the repressed, giving a voice to those some sought to silence.

So if you're asked why Twitter matters, you can tell people that, at its heart, Twitter is about leveraging the specialisation of our species. So even if we each take a different road, we all reach the
55 destination of wisdom together.

Question ?

7 Both writers express their views on Twitter. Identify key areas on which they disagree. In your answer, you should refer in detail to both passages.

You may answer this question in continuous prose or in a series of developed bullet points. **(5)**

Answers

These suggestions are not marking instructions. The range of answers that follow offer possible answers, with advice on the general approach to the task.

1 Word choice:
   - 'claim' (used twice) suggests that these facts are unsubstantiated.
   - 'can't be bothered' suggests many people show indifference to such things as Facebook.
   - 'manage without' suggests people don't find it at all necessary.
   - 'still eludes' suggests that universal coverage slips away and can't be grasped.
   - 'behave as though all the world' – 'as though' casts doubt on the truth of the statement that 'all the world' is involved.
   - 'grandiose' – exaggerated.
   - 'evangelical' – zeal to spread the word over the whole human world.

Sentence structure:
   - The declarative (or summative) short sentence 'Ubiquity still eludes the social media' suggests the writer's confidence in this statement that the social media have not succeeded. (You may not know what 'ubiquity' means, although the context might help you to work it out; but that need not stop you from noticing the short sentence and its probable function.)
   - The use of the colon in line 9 – 'as pithily:' introduces an expansion of the idea which makes clear in an economical way that the writer thinks Twitter's claims are still very far from being true.
   - The inverted commas round 'active' could possibly seem as casting some sort of criticism of the practice itself, as if writing 140 character messages were lazy and inactive.

Another possibility:
   - The use of statistics to prove his point certainly seem to be conclusive – only 215 million out of a world population of 7.2 billion, which is a tiny percentage (0.029% actually, not that you would be expected to work that out – it's not an arithmetic paper you are sitting!).

⇒

You have been asked to consider at least two features, so an answer that depended entirely on word choice (for example) could not gain full marks.

Remember that if you simply quote the word or phrase (such as 'grandiose') or simply identify a feature (such as 'use of colon') without making a sensible comment on its effect, you will gain no marks. Any four of these 11 points with a sensible comment should gain you at least 1 mark each – possibly more if the point is well developed.

There may well be other features such as tone or paragraphing – the single sentence opening paragraph – and so on: there is no list of features, and so you are free to deal with any language feature you can identify.

2 a) • Only a very few people have the ability to say anything meaningful in 140 letters, so it's not worth reading most of the messages.
   • Lots of people use it only to boast about themselves/to abuse others/to promote dodgy political ideas.

These answers have been careful to use their own words but when it comes to something like 'politics' used in this sequence, there is little point in trying to translate it into something less precise like 'sociological, democratic processes' … life is too short!

b) Sentence structure:
   • Parallel structure of the two sentences beginning 'The number' allows you to appreciate the tiny size of the 'good' as against the massive number of the 'bad'.
   • The two uses of parenthesis (it is) and (it isn't) again allows you to make the contrast between the two types.
   • The short first sentence is a dismissive summing up of his reasons for avoiding Twitter.
   • The short last sentence is also dismissive – it is obvious to the writer that Twitter is of little interest.

Word choice:
   • 'vanishingly small' suggests that the number of those who would be worth communicating with is so small that it becomes difficult even to see them as they disappear into the distance.
   • 'self-promotion' suggests bombastic people are best avoided.
   • 'nastiness' suggests spite – a desire to make someone uncomfortable.

Imagery:
   • 'the typographic equivalent of A SHRIEK' suggests that the use of things like capital letters to emphasise that these tweets just ends up sounding as if the letters themselves are literally 'shouting' at you.

Tone:
   • is dismissive/superior – he thinks his opinion is better. This is shown by such things as '(it is)', '(it isn't)'.

Typography:
   • 'A SHRIEK' is a typographic device to demonstrate what he is talking about – over-emphasis.

Any of these ten points with a sensible comment should gain you at least 1 mark each – possibly more if the point is well developed.

But remember that if you simply quote the word or phrase (such as 'nastiness') or simply identify a feature (such as 'use of parenthesis') without making a sensible comment on its effect, you will gain no marks.

⇒

In this question there is a list of suggested features to help you with your answer by reminding you of them – and it is pretty certain that you will find examples of these features. It is, however, an open list and so you are free to notice other features such as the typography.

3 ● to avoid letting the bullies go unchallenged.
   ● to uphold the idea that people should be free to speak their minds.
   ● because it is not going to go away/ignoring the new world of digital communication won't stop it.

These three points would gain 3 marks. Note that in this kind of question you have to remember the assumption that you have to 'use your own words'.

4 a) ● He feels he is being left behind because everyone else belongs to Twitter.
   ● 2014 is going to be important to journalists so he doesn't want to miss things.
   ● Twitter is a place where discussion will happen.

Any two of these for 2 marks.

b) Word choice:
   ● 'less elevated reasons' suggests that he was almost ashamed of his giving in to the pressure.
   ● 'ramshackle' suggests that although active, the structure is likely to topple over.
   ● 'the badlands of the Wild West' suggests that the debate is a free-for-all without any rules.
   ● 'Periclean Athens' suggests the civilised debates in ancient Athens in a controlled and structured environment.
   ● 'staggeringly fast' suggests that one of the virtues of Twitter is that word spreads unbelievably quickly – possibly before waiting for verification.
   ● 'flawed' suggests that everything is not always true.

   Imagery:
   ● 'herd thundering through' suggests that the rush to join Twitter is as mindless as cattle stampeding, and just as unstoppable, but that he is being carried along by it almost against his will.

   Contrast:
   ● Contrast between the Wild West and Ancient Athens shows the two contrary sides of Twitter.
   ● Contrast between 'fast' and 'flawed' shows the good and the bad.

   Sentence structure:
   ● The use of the colon in line 30 'less elevated reasons:' introduces the reason – everyone else was already there. It shows the pressure he felt to conform.

You have been given no specific number of features and the list of features is 'open', so you are free to make comment on any aspect of language you notice.

But, you are asked to deal with his 'conflicting feelings', so there must be at least one reference and comment on each side of the conflict – his 'good' feelings and his 'bad' feelings.

One of the suggested features is 'contrast': this is meant to be a helpful suggestion to remind you of the need to look at both sides.

Any four of these ten points with a sensible comment should gain you at least 1 mark each – possibly more if the point is well developed, so long as at least one reference is made to each side. But remember that if you simply quote the word or phrase (such as 'ramshackle') or simply identify a feature (such as 'use of contrast') without making a sensible comment on its effect, you will gain no marks.

5 ● The writer concludes his discussion of Twitter by returning to one of his initial points – that it is a forum for some rather unpleasant people – 'nastiness' and 'threats of rape and death'. He states in the same paragraph that the number of people of bad intent is 'staggering' in volume.

 ● Although he does mention some advantages of Twitter in lines 26–45, he returns to his original criticisms in lines 55–60, which makes an effective ending to his argument about Twitter by leaving the reader with an unpleasant impression of it.

 ● The use of pejorative words/phrases/imagery is brought to a climax by the language of the last sentence: 'the witless and the worst flocking, much as dank, cosy shadows attract cockroaches'. The simile comparing some Twitter users to 'cockroaches' suggests really unpleasant people, thriving in unwholesome darkness, creating mould and deterioration.

 ● This recalls his descriptions earlier on of 'scum' suggesting the filthy surface of stagnant water, and 'thugs' suggesting an unintelligent use of brute strength to destroy other people.

This answer includes both ideas and language features, and is more detailed than would be necessary. Any of these attempts or any combination of the individual points would gain 2 marks.

6 ● New digital technology has been blamed for reducing the time that people appear to be able to concentrate for.

 ● His theory, on the contrary, is that people just don't pay much attention to what they read and hear anyway.

 ● But possibly the whole pace and bombardment of information is too much for our brains – although this theory has not been proved.

 ● But, finally, the kind of knowledge gained in this way is ultimately too superficial to be of much use.

It is likely that each of these four paragraphs will provide you with a 'topic' point. 'Explain' implies making some sort of connection – 'on the contrary', 'but', 'but finally'. Remember to use your own words throughout.

7 ● There is no need to set out your answer in a table like the one on the next page. It is laid out here to clarify the ideas in these particular passages. You should find your own way of answering this question. Look at the foot of the table for further advice.

Areas of disagreement		
	Passage 1	Passage 2
1 Quantity of knowledge	Very few have anything useful to pass on – vanishingly small.	Increases our knowledge/potential to enlighten us.
2 Quality of knowledge	The type of knowledge passed on by Twitter is essentially shallow/dumbing down – self-promotion, nastiness, pursuing political points.	Tool for distilling understanding in the most digestible form.
3 Attitude to others	Twitter increases our ability to abuse each other – anonymous threats.	Sharing of information is a joy – something special to say.
4 Promoting communication	Twitter gives a voice to the pompous and nasty – people you would cross the street to avoid.	Twitter gives an empowering voice to the repressed/spawns communities who lend members mutual support.
5 Facts versus wisdom	Twitter knowledge is not worth having – information is grazed/attention flits like a butterfly.	Allows us to reach the destination of wisdom/hastening the specialisation of our species.

There is some area of overlap among these points – 2 and 5 are quite similar, but 2 is dealing with the inherent worth or quality of the knowledge whereas 5 is dealing with each writer's conclusion about the worth of the knowledge to the human race.

In this kind of question you may be asked to look for a specific number of points but, if not, you should probably be looking for three or four key areas.

One way of starting might be to write down the three or four key areas you have found. You could then accumulate the evidence from each of the passages to back up each of these key areas. Or you might take each key area in turn and give the relevant supporting evidence.

You can use bullet points or you can write a short paragraph to set out your evidence.

It is helpful to identify quite clearly where the first of your key points ends and the next one begins. It helps you to keep your ideas in order and perhaps prevents you from making the same point twice.

Chapter 5

Critical Reading

This is the second exam paper that you have to sit in your external exam. You have 1 hour and 30 minutes to complete two tasks:

Section 1: 20 marks

Read an extract from a Scottish text or a Scottish poem (or an extract from a Scottish poem) from the list specified and attempt the questions.

Section 2: 20 marks

Write one critical essay on a previously studied text from Drama, Prose, Poetry, Film and TV Drama or Language Study.

There are two other restrictions on what you can and can't do.

1 You must not use the same **text** twice.
2 Each of your answers must be on a different **genre**.

For example, if you have answered on Scottish poetry in Section 1, you cannot write your critical essay on poetry of any kind, Scottish or from anywhere else in the world.

How you approach your choice will depend on which texts you have been taught and which you have prepared for the exam. For example:

1 You might have been taught one specified Scottish text and one or more texts from outside the list, in different genres.
2 You might have been taught two specified Scottish texts and one or more texts from outside the list, each in a different genre.
3 You might have been taught three or more specified Scottish texts in different genres taken from the specified list.

If you have prepared two or three specified Scottish texts then you obviously should look at both Section 1 and Section 2 questions before you make your choice, but even if you have only studied one Scottish text – and therefore have no choice in Section 1 – you might like to look at the following advice.

There is some psychological evidence to suggest that if you very quickly scan the questions in Section 2 before getting down to answering Section 1, then some part of your brain can work away at clarifying your choice for Section 2 while the 'active' part of your brain is busy answering the questions in Section 1. You might like to try this to see if it works for you. Remember, however, that time is very tight in the Critical Reading paper.

Section 1 is where your choice of text is limited to the list of Scottish texts. You must answer on **one** of the 14 texts presented to you in the paper.

Your choice of text in Section 1 limits your choice of **genre** in Section 2.

The best way to illustrate this, rather than dealing in abstract 'ifs', is to look at aspects of Critical Essay choices (see pages 146–9) once you have clearly understood the requirements for Section 1.

Section 1: Scottish text

There are two important pieces of advice that apply to all the following examples of Scottish text questions:

1 Lots of the work you have done on Understanding, Analysis and Evaluation in Chapter 4 of this book is applicable to the questions on the Scottish text you choose for Section 1. For example, always check the mark allocation:

   Two marks are awarded for each detailed/insightful comment plus a reference. One mark is awarded for each more basic comment plus a reference. Therefore, it is possible to achieve 4 marks with two detailed comments (plus references) but if you are not sure whether your comments are detailed/insightful enough, don't stop at two.

2 The list of features mentioned in the boxes that precede each of the genres in Section 2 of the exam paper will remind you of the kind of things you may wish to consider when answering the questions in Section 1.

In an English course, nothing is wasted. All the skills are transferrable!

Hints & tips

If you haven't already done so, read the Introduction at the start of this book, because it gives you useful advice on how to use this book effectively.

Note about answers

There are three important points to make about the answers:

1 These are possible answers – not the only answers.
2 There are many more points contained in these answers than you would need to produce for a given question. Look at the mark allocation and see how many points you will have to make. For example, in a 4-mark question, this gives you an opportunity to gain marks as 1+1+1+1 or 2+2 or 2+1+1.
3 The **commentaries on the answers** are even more important than the answers themselves because they show the method of arriving at a good answer.

Note: it is not always repeated in every answer but:

1 A reference alone gains no marks. A basic comment is worth 1 mark, whereas a detailed, insightful comment can be worth 2 marks.
2 You must use your own words as far as possible: you should make clear you know the meaning of complex words; simple words can obviously be repeated without trying to find a synonym.

Poetry

Poetry is probably the best genre to start with as (most of) the texts are short and self-contained, so we can look at a complete example.

You might think also that poetry is easier than prose or drama because the texts are shorter – the six poems listed for Norman MacCaig amount to only 155 lines, for example. But you have to know these poems so well that you can quote readily from all of them. You will have one poem in front of you in the paper, for which you can gain the first 10 marks. The other 10 marks are available for your ability to relate this poem to at least one other suitable poem by MacCaig in answer to a question you will have been asked.

There are **two** possible types of poetry texts you may be asked to deal with here. The first is a **complete poem**, e.g. 'Originally' by Carol Ann Duffy (see below), and the second is **an extract from a longer poem**, e.g. from 'Mrs Midas' by Carol Ann Duffy (pages 105–106).

There are also **three** kinds of final 10-mark questions:

1 One kind is concerned with identifying a **common theme or central concern**.
2 The second kind is concerned with the use of a **similar technique or set of techniques**.
3 The third kind comments on **character or relationships** (often in combination with a theme or central concern).

Poetry A: a complete poem

Originally

We came from our own country in a red room

which fell through the fields, our mother singing

our father's name to the turn of the wheels.

My brothers cried, one of them bawling, *Home,*

5 *Home,* as the miles rushed back to the city,

the street, the house, the vacant rooms

where we didn't live any more. I stared

at the eyes of a blind toy, holding its paw.

All childhood is an emigration. Some are slow,

10 leaving you standing, resigned, up an avenue

where no one you know stays. Others are sudden.

Your accent wrong. Corners, which seem familiar,

leading to unimagined pebble-dashed estates, big boys

eating worms and shouting words you don't understand.

15 My parents' anxiety stirred like a loose tooth

in my head. *I want our own country,* I said.

But then you forget, or don't recall, or change,

and, seeing your brother swallow a slug, feel only

a skelf of shame. I remember my tongue

20 shedding its skin like a snake, my voice

in the classroom sounding just like the rest. Do I only think

I lost a river, culture, speech, sense of first space

and the right place? Now, *Where do you come from?*

strangers ask. *Originally?* And I hesitate.

Carol Ann Duffy

Hints & tips ★

*If you have a choice between this Scottish text and another, you should look carefully at **all** the questions asked on **this poem**. You may be quite happy with the choice of 'Originally' because it is a poem you know well and have enjoyed. Questions 1, 2 and 3 may be fine, but question 4 — which is worth 10 marks — asks about the idea of 'the outsider'. The problem is deciding which other poem or poems by Carol Ann Duffy explore this theme — and do you know them well enough to find relevant references for your answer? You should **always** have looked at Section 2 before making your choice.*

Questions

1 By referring closely to verse 1 (lines 1–8), analyse the use of language to describe the feelings of the speaker. **(2)**
2 By referring to at least two examples, analyse the use of language that helps to convey the anxieties hinted at in verse 2 (lines 9–16). **(4)**
3 How do the ideas of the last section of the poem from 'Do I only …' to the end (lines 21–24) justify the choice of 'Originally' as the title of the poem? You should refer to at least two examples. **(4)**
4 By referring to this poem and at least one other by Carol Ann Duffy, show how the idea of the outsider is explored in her poetry. **(10)**

Answer

This section takes you through a set of possible answers. Remember, though, that there will be many other equally acceptable answers.

1 **By referring closely to verse 1 (lines 1–8), analyse the use of language to describe the feelings of the speaker. (2)**

There are several possibilities:

- word choice: 'own country'
- imagery: 'fell through the fields'
- imagery: 'the miles rushed back'
- climax/anti-climax: 'the city, the street, the house, the vacant rooms'
- word choice: 'vacant rooms'
- word choice: 'stared' or 'blind toy' or 'holding its paw'.

It would be difficult to use evidence from lines 3 and 4 because they are about the parents and the brothers, not the poet.

It is better to be as specific as you can in your answer. If you choose word choice, you might look at the connotations of two of the words mentioned above. If imagery, you could look in close detail at one or two of the images. Climax has only one example but a satisfactory explanation of how it worked would provide a good answer.

Look at the allocation of marks. There are 2 marks for this question, so it would be foolish to mention every technique you identify. Two good examples should gain the 2 marks.

Avoid taking a long blanket quotation, covering a lot of the words, and making a generalised comment about technique without specifying exactly what you are talking about.

For example:

- Reference: 'I stared/at the eyes of a blind toy, holding its paw.'
- Comment: The word choice makes you feel that the poet is sad, and needs to be comforted.

The weakness of this answer is that it is too generalised to gain any credit. The comment is true but no specific analysis has been done.

Exercise 1

Take each of the suggested references in this list (except 'vacant rooms') and provide a relevant comment on each, linking it to the poet's feelings.

(Answers on page 129.)

Hints & tips ⭐

*Remember, as in the Reading for Understanding, Analysis and Evaluation Paper, it is not enough to identify the words, phrases, technique or feature you have chosen; you must show **how** these words, phrases or techniques are effective in showing us the poet's feelings. There is no mark for simple identification. For example, if you say that the word choice of 'vacant rooms' is effective, and nothing more, you have not really analysed the phrase. You would have to comment on the connotations of 'vacant', which suggests an emptiness, a lack of the people who once lived there – a sort of abandonment. This shows the poet's feelings of loss and regret.*

Exercise 2 ✏️

Take each of the suggested references in the list of bullet points in the answer to question 2 below (except the loose tooth image) and provide a relevant comment on each, linking it to 'anxieties'.

(Answers on page 129.)

Answers

2 **By referring to at least two examples, analyse the use of language that helps to convey the anxieties hinted at in verse 2 (lines 9–16). (4)**
   The most obvious choices here are imagery and word choice:
   ● Imagery: 'All childhood is an emigration', 'anxiety stirred like a loose tooth in my head'.
   ● Word choice: 'resigned', 'unimagined', 'big boys eating worms', 'don't understand' (these are the most obvious ones, but other possibilities exist).
   You could also talk about:
   ● Contrast: 'some are slow'/'others are sudden'.
   ● The use of direct speech.
   You are being offered 4 marks for this question, and you must deal with at least two examples. So, you have the choice of dealing with four examples in a basic way, or you could deal with fewer in more depth. Remember that simply identifying the image is not enough. There has to be a comment on its effectiveness in exploring 'anxieties'.
   For example:
   'anxiety stirred like a loose tooth in my head' uses a simile to suggest the constant nagging of the worries the poet has and her inability to forget them, in the same way that your tongue keeps finding out and disturbing a loose tooth.

3 **How do the ideas of the last section of the poem from 'Do I only …' to the end (lines 21–24) justify the choice of 'Originally' as the title of the poem? (4)**
   This question is really about the effectiveness of a conclusion – a concept you have already looked at in Reading for Understanding, Analysis and Evaluation on pages 47–49.
   You must link the ideas in these lines with the idea of 'Originally'. The most obvious tie-up is that 'Originally?' is used as a question in the last line, showing that the poem has been an illustration of how hard a question that is to answer. The ideas of 'first space' refer back to the first verse with its references to vacant rooms, and the city, street and house that Duffy left as a child. The question as to whether she
   ⇨

really has lost her cultural roots is now not clear to her – 'Do I only think …?' shows the doubt. Therefore, the answer to the question as to where she comes from 'originally' is now obscured by time – 'then you forget, or don't recall' such things as changing her accent and blending into her new background.

4 **By referring to this poem and at least one other by Carol Ann Duffy, show how the idea of the outsider is explored in her poetry. (10)**

*To make sure you answer all the parts of this last question you should do **three** things:*

A *You should show how your understanding of the idea of 'the outsider' has been developed.*

B *Next you should show how the idea of 'the outsider' has been dealt with in the text in front of you.*

C *You should then develop more fully the theme of the outsider. You would be expected to make reference to suitable poem(s) you have studied. In this case 'War Photographer' could provide the material you need.*

For example:

A In Duffy's poetry, an outsider can be seen as someone who is divorced from their roots and finds it difficult to relate to a new set of customs and values. (1) The outsider might feel isolated from those around when his/her own experience and values are different, as when the photographer feels removed from the people back home at home in 'War Photographer'. (1)

B 'Originally' is about being uprooted from her place of birth and her distress as a child; she needs the comfort of 'holding its paw'. There is a lack of a sense of identity in the last two lines – 'And I hesitate'.

C *You would be expected to make references to the other poetry you have chosen to look at, showing how it contributes to the idea that the speaker is an outsider.*

You can answer this question either by bullet points or by use of a series of linked statements. You may find that the bullet point method helps you to structure your answer more clearly, or you may find that linked statements allow you to incorporate your comments more easily. You should use whichever method works for you. Both of these methods are shown below.

Bullet points

- Belfast. Beirut. Phnom Penh. The mention of foreign and war-torn locations suggests a separation from his own country's calmer and more settled environment, contrasted with 'Rural England'.
- 'He has a job to do'/'to do what someone must' shows that he is somehow set outside society and is doing a job that others would not be keen on doing because of having to witness the pain.
- Blood stained foreign dust again emphasises the geographical separation that isolates him from natives of his own country.
- 'A hundred agonies/pick out five or six' suggests that the society he comes back to with his hundred photographs will only be shown a selection – a selection that has just been 'picked out' seemingly at random and not chosen carefully. Society will never know the full force of the horror he has witnessed – 'how the blood stained into foreign dust'.
- 'between bath and the pre-lunch beers' – society is affected by his photographs only temporarily; he is different – the knowledge is permanent.
- 'he earns a living and they do not care' ends the poem, definitively showing his isolation.

Series of linked statements

In 'War Photographer', the photographer's job sets him apart from the rest of society. He is 'alone' and 'has a job to do', which is to communicate the suffering he has witnessed in war zones such as

Belfast and Beirut – 'how the blood stained into foreign dust'. The developing photographs remind him of the horrors he has seen and how he 'must' show the violence so that people at home will be moved to think about foreign wars and atrocities. But his isolation from the society that surrounds him is emphasised by the fact that, on the whole, society does not want to know. In fact, only a tiny selection of his work will be allowed to have an effect – his 'editor will pick out five or six'. The fact that 'pick out' is used instead of 'choose' shows that even the selection is slightly random, not carefully thought through. The photographs only have a temporary effect on the readers whose 'eyeballs prick with tears between bath and pre-lunch beers', whereas the effect on him is more lasting – as a result he has to steel himself against the emotion – 'stares impassively'. The last line – 'he earns a living and they do not care' – shows finally the gulf between him and the rest of society and how he is isolated because of what he has seen, but which he can only communicate in part.

In this 10-mark question, there are up to 2 marks available for part A, up to 2 marks for part B and up to 6 marks for part C. You could gain these by making six basic points, three detailed/insightful points, or a combination of these. You have to select relevant references and link them to the idea of 'the outsider'.

There is a lot to remember in poetry answers such as these, but you have had the advantage of tackling these poems in detail in class, so you should know them well enough to make relevant and accurate references to them in your responses to this kind of question.

Other poems from the selection could also be used; for example, 'Mrs Midas' deals with her relationship with her husband who becomes an outsider as a result of his foolish (she says selfish) wish which has destroyed their intimacy.

Poetry B: an extract from a longer poem

Mrs Midas

It was late September. I'd just poured a glass of wine, begun
to unwind, while the vegetables cooked. The kitchen
filled with the smell of itself, relaxed, its steamy breath
gently blanching the windows. So I opened one,
5   then with my fingers wiped the other's glass like a brow.
He was standing under the pear tree snapping a twig.

Now the garden was long and the visibility poor, the way
the dark of the ground seems to drink the light of the sky,
but that twig in his hand was gold. And then he plucked
10   a pear from a branch – we grew Fondante d'Automne –
and it sat in his palm, like a lightbulb. On.
I thought to myself, Is he putting fairy lights in the tree?

He came into the house. The doorknobs gleamed.
He drew the blinds. You know the mind; I thought of

Hints & tips

If you have a choice between this Scottish text and another, you should look carefully at all the questions asked on this poem. You may be quite happy with the choice of 'Mrs Midas', but always look at the last question (in this case, question 4) to see how easily it allows you to show your knowledge of the selection of poems you have read. Before you make up your mind finally, you should always have looked at Section 2 before making your choice.

15 the Field of the Cloth of Gold and of Miss Macready.

He sat in that chair like a king on a burnished throne.

The look on his face was strange, wild, vain. I said,

What in the name of God is going on? He started to laugh.

I served up the meal. For starters, corn on the cob.

20 Within seconds he was spitting out the teeth of the rich.

He toyed with his spoon, then mine, then with the knives, the forks.

He asked where was the wine. I poured with a shaking hand,

a fragrant, bone-dry white from Italy, then watched

as he picked up the glass, goblet, golden chalice, drank.

25 It was then that I started to scream.

Carol Ann Duffy

Questions ❓

1 Analyse the use of language to create mood in verse 1. **(2)**
2 By referring to at least two examples, show in what ways the language of verse 4 is effective in building up to the climax 'It was then that I started to scream'. **(4)**
3 Analyse aspects of the language or structure in this extract which create a believable narrative voice for the speaker. You should refer to at least two examples. **(4)**
4 By referring to this extract and at least one other poem by Carol Ann Duffy, show how effectively she explores the joys and sorrows of a close relationship. **(10)**

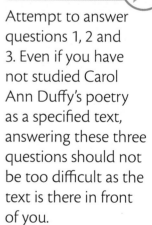

Exercise 3

Attempt to answer questions 1, 2 and 3. Even if you have not studied Carol Ann Duffy's poetry as a specified text, answering these three questions should not be too difficult as the text is there in front of you.

(Answers on pages 129–130.)

Answer

This section takes you through a possible answer to question 4. Remember, though, that there will be many other equally acceptable answers.

4 **By referring to this extract and at least one other poem by Carol Ann Duffy, show how effectively she explores the joys and sorrows of a close relationship. (10)**

*To make sure you answer all the parts of this last question you must do **three** things:*

A *You should show how your understanding of the joys and sorrows of a close relationship have been developed.*

B *Next you should show how the idea of the close relationship has been dealt with in 'Mrs Midas'.*

C *For the 6 additional marks available you need to refer to the idea of the joys and sorrows of a close relationship in one (or more than one) of the other poems by Carol Ann Duffy you have studied. In this case 'Valentine' could provide the material needed.*

For example:

A In Duffy's poetry, the joys and sorrows of a relationship are ever-present and can tip quickly from one state of pleasurable anticipation and deep happiness to its reverse. (1) When a speaker in a poem discusses a relationship, the typical symbols of love can be seen as inadequate and clichéd or even menacing. (1)

B In 'Mrs Midas' the warmth of the kitchen, the relaxation and anticipation of a happy, contented evening – 'begun to unwind' – is destroyed. The sorrowful side of the relationship is dealt with in the increasing horror of the consequences of this 'gift' – Midas 'strange, wild, vain' turning to destruction – 'spitting out the teeth of the rich' and even worse, the change of 'glass, goblet, golden chalice' with the horror of what might happen to the wine.

C *You would be expected to make references to the other poetry you have chosen to look at – in this case, 'Valentine' – showing the idea of the joys and sorrows of a close relationship. You can answer this question either by the use of bullet points or in a series of linked statements. You may find that the bullet point method helps you to structure your answer more clearly, or you may find that linked statements allow you to incorporate your comments more easily. You should use whichever method works for you. Both of these methods are shown below.*

Bullet points

- 'Not a red rose or a satin heart/I give you an onion' seems to show two opposites – a red rose is usually symbolic of love and an onion is known to give rise to tears.
- 'Not a cute card or a kissogram/I give you an onion' goes further and suggests that the usual Valentine stuff is worthless and that the onion symbolises something more sincere, but which can cause deep emotion – not all the feelings are joyful, though.
- 'Possessive and faithful' sounds quite optimistic, but it is followed by 'for as long as we are', which suggests that maybe it is not permanent.
- The last lines seem to say that a wedding ring can be lethal, connected with the onion scent on the knife used to cut it into rings – a wedding ring.
- The overall impression of the poem is that love can be strong and violent, 'fierce kiss', but also tender and soft, 'light/like the careful undressing of love'.

⇨

Series of linked statements

In 'Valentine', there is sorrow about a troubled love – a love that might be lost in the future. The 'red rose' and 'satin heart' are ignored in favour of an onion, which first promises the joys of a loving relationship – 'It promises light/like the careful undressing of love'. The onion seems to become next a symbol of truth, even though the truth can be painful – 'a wobbling photo of grief'. The 'cute card or a kissogram' are seen to be trivial, not representing the strong passion they have; 'fierce kiss will stay on your lips', but then the ambivalence becomes apparent again – 'possessive' sounds more damaging than 'faithful' and 'for as long as we are' could signal the end of the affair. The last lines seem to say that a wedding ring can be lethal, connected with the onion scent on the knife used to cut it into rings – a wedding ring.

The overall impression of the poem is that love can be strong and violent ('fierce kiss'), but also tender and soft ('light/like the careful undressing of love').

In this 10-mark question, there are up to 2 marks available for part A, up to 2 marks for part B and up to 6 marks for part C. You could gain these by making six basic points, three detailed/insightful points, or a combination of these. You have to select relevant references and link them to the idea of the joys and sorrows of a close relationship.

There is a lot to remember in poetry answers such as these, but you have had the advantage of tackling these poems in detail in class, so you should know them well enough to make relevant and accurate references to them in your responses to this kind of question.

There are several poems within the specified list that would suit the question.

Prose

Short story

The short story option from the specified Scottish texts has some of the advantages and some of the drawbacks that have already been described in the Poetry section.

The total scope of all four stories in each of the selections (George Mackay Brown and Iain Crichton Smith) is only just over 12,000 words – much shorter than a novel or a play. But again you need to have a detailed knowledge of all four of the stories for the writer you have been taught. You will be presented with an extract from one of the stories, which you have to relate to at least one other story.

There are **three** kinds of final *10-mark* questions:

1 One kind is concerned with identifying a **common theme or central concern**.
2 The second kind is concerned with the use of a **similar technique or set of techniques**.
3 The third kind comments on **character or relationships** (often in combination with a theme or central concern).

This short story by Iain Crichton Smith illustrates the third type.

Home (extract)

Hints & tips

If you have a choice between this Scottish text and another, you should look carefully at **all** the questions asked on **this story**. You may be quite happy with the choice of 'Home' but always look at the last question (in this case, question 4) to see how easily it allows you to show your knowledge of another short story by Iain Crichton Smith. Before you make up your mind finally, you should **always** have looked at Section 2 before making your choice.

'All right, boys,' he said in an ingratiating voice. 'We're going anyway. We've seen all we want.'

'Did you hear that, Micky? He's seen all he wants to see. Would you say that was an insult?' Micky gazed benevolently at him

5 through a lot of hair.

'Depends. What have you seen, daddy?'

'I used to live here,' he said jovially. 'In the old days. The best years of my life.' The words rang hollow between them.

'Hear that?' said Micky. 'Hear him. He's left us. Daddy's left us.'

10 He came up close and said quietly,

'Get out of here, daddy, before we cut you up, and take your camera and your bus with us. And your bag too. Right?'

The one with the curving moustache spat and said quietly 'Tourist.'

He got into the car beside his still unsmiling wife who was still
15 staring straight ahead of her. The car gathered speed and made its way down the main street. In the mirror he could see the brown tenement diminishing. The thin stringy woman was still at the window looking out, screaming at the children.

The shops along both sides of the street were all changed.
20 There used to be a road down to the river and the lavatories ⇨

⇨

but he couldn't see anything there now. Later on he passed a new yellow petrol station, behind a miniature park with a blue bench on it.

'Mind we used to take the bus out past here?' he said, looking
25 towards the woods on their right, where all the secret shades were, and the squirrels leaped.

The sky was darkening and the light seemed concentrated ahead of them in steely rays.

Suddenly he said,

30 'I wish to God we were home.'

She smiled for the first time. But he was still thinking of the scarred tenement and of what he should have said to these youths. Punks. He should have said, 'This is my home too. More than yours. You're just passing through.'

35 Punks with Edwardian moustaches. By God, if they were in Africa they would be sorted out. A word in the ear of the Chief Inspector over a cigar and that would be it. By God, they knew how to deal with punks where he came from.

He thought of razor-suited Jamieson setting out on a Friday night
40 in his lone battle with the Catholics. Where was he now? Used to be a boiler-man or something. By God, he would have sorted them out. And his wife used to clean the cinema steps on those draughty winter days.

'So you admit you were wrong,' said his wife.

45 He drove on, accelerating past a smaller car and blaring his horn savagely. There was no space in this bloody country. Everyone crowded together like rats.

'Here, look at that,' he said, 'that didn't used to be there.' It was a big building, probably a hospital.

50 'Remember we used to come down here on the bus,' he said. 'That didn't used to be here.'

He drove into the small town and got out of the car to stretch. The yellow lights rayed the road and the cafés had red globes above them. He could hardly recognise the place.

55 'We'd better find a hotel,' he said.

His wife's face brightened.

They stopped at the Admiral and were back home when the boy in the blue uniform with the yellow edgings took their rich brown leather cases.

Iain Crichton Smith

Questions ?

1 Analyse how tone is used effectively in the dialogue between the man and the two youths (lines 1–13). You should refer to **at least two** examples. **(4)**
2 Analyse the contribution of line 30 to the structure and theme of the extract. **(2)**
3 Read lines 45–54. By referring to **at least two** examples, analyse how the language of these lines shows the man's discomfiture at his surroundings. **(4)**
4 By referring to this story and to one other by Iain Crichton Smith, discuss his presentation of uneasy relationships. **(10)**

Answers

This section takes you through possible answers to these questions. Remember, though, that there will be many other equally acceptable answers.

1 **Analyse how tone is used effectively in the dialogue between the man and the two youths (lines 1–13). You should refer to at least two examples. (4)**
   - 'ingratiating' suggests the man is being defensive, trying to avert a confrontation.
   - 'Would you say that was an insult?' suggests a still menacing tone – that the man has not succeeded in getting out of the situation.
   - 'jovially' (especially when combined with 'rang hollow') suggests a forced attempt to turn the situation to a friendly basis.
   - Repetition of 'hear that', 'Hear him' and 'left us' suggests mockery on the part of the youths, who know they have the upper hand.
   - 'quietly' when uttering threats is more menacing than shouting would be.
   - 'Tourist' said quietly suggests that the youth despises him as a 'poverty tourist'.

   You are being offered 4 marks in this question, and you must deal with at least two examples. So, you have the choice of dealing with four examples in a basic way, or you could deal with fewer in more depth.

2 **Analyse the contribution of line 30 to the structure and theme of the extract. (2)**
   - This line marks a turning point in the incident between the man trying hard to connect with his previous life and finding that it doesn't work – he has no place there.
   - The ambiguous use of 'home' – does he mean his past physical home, or his actual present financial and social 'home' where he feels in control and comfortable?

   Either of these comments would be worth 2 marks; or both commented on more simply for 1 mark each.

3 **Read lines 45–54. By referring to at least two examples, analyse how the language of these lines shows the man's discomfiture at his surroundings. (4)**
   - 'blaring … savagely'
   - 'crowded like rats'
   - 'that didn't used to be here'
   - 'yellow lights rayed'
   - 'red globes'
   - 'hardly recognise'

   A fully developed comment on any of the above could gain 2 marks. A simpler answer might get 1 mark. You would be commenting on word choice, imagery, tone …
   For example, a developed answer:
   'blaring … savagely' effectively gives an impression of the volume of the sound – loud and brassy, and the emotion of the driver being out of control, wanting to inflict harm on someone.

⇨

A simple answer:

'blaring … savagely' gives the impression that the man makes his car make a loud noise because he is feeling violent. (*This comment attempts to deal only with the connotations of 'savagely'.*)

4 **By referring to this story and to one other by Iain Crichton Smith, discuss his presentation of uneasy relationships. (10)**

   *To make sure you answer all parts of this question you must do **three** things:*

   A *You should show your understanding of a relationship that is strained by uncomfortable social circumstances.*

   B *Next you should show, by referring to the extract, how the relationship between the man and his wife (or possibly between the youths and the man – although that would be far more difficult) is an uneasy one.*

   C *For the additional six marks available you need to show how Crichton Smith presents another uneasy relationship in one of his short stories.*

   For example:

   A In Crichton Smith's stories, relationships are often uneasy because of the cultural environment, which can create pressures such as the wartime stress in 'The Telegram' (1) or because of conflict between the priorities and attitudes of the characters. as with the husband and wife in 'Home'. (1)

   B The wife's disapproval of the whole outing into the past is shown in 'his still unsmiling wife' and she remains unsmiling through his attempt to interest her in the woods they used to know until he finally capitulates and admits that the enterprise has been a mistake: 'I wish to God we were home.' At this admission the wife smiles 'for the first time' but when she tries to get him to make the confession explicit he persists in trying to interest her still in their surroundings. It's only when he suggests a hotel (civilisation) that she is finally satisfied. (*The uneasy relationship between the man and the two youths could also be referred to here.*)

   C *In this case, there is an uneasy relationship in 'The Telegram' and also in 'Mother and Son', so either of these stories would provide material for answering this question.*

   The remaining six marks are available for reference to the uneasy relationship in one of these stories. You may write your answer to this question either as a series of linked statements, or as a list of bullet points. Both of these methods are shown below for the relationship in 'The Telegram'.

You can answer this question either by bullet points, or by use of a series of linked statements. You may find that the bullet point method helps you to structure your answer more clearly, or you may find that linked statements allow you to incorporate your comments more easily. You should use which ever method works for you.

Series of linked statements

The relationship between the fat woman and the thin woman (who are neighbours) is initially one of putting up with each other despite their differences. The uneasiness is born of social and personality differences. The fat woman is resentful of what she sees as the snobbish adherence to education, which has allowed the thin woman's son to go to university and become an officer – her 'son had to salute the thin woman's son', as he is of a lower rank. The thin woman resents the fat woman as she feels left out of the community because she was an incomer, and her 'pretensions' were not understood – nor were the sacrifices she had made to achieve her goal. She resents the easy-going nature of the fat woman who (lazily) lets her cow roam. When the elder appears along the street with the telegram, their relationship becomes closer out of a need for mutual support. The fat woman is terrified when her house is next. She doesn't want to show her weakness in front of the thin woman but is surprised by the joy of 'the arm of the thin woman' round her shoulders. She suppresses the desire to dance for joy when her house is passed, admires the firmness of the thin woman when they both believe that the news must be about the thin woman's son and begins to understand the sacrifice she had made. When the elder passes, they both realise that they are 'safe' and the relationship turns cold again: 'They drank their tea in silence turning away from each other'. Crichton Smith's presentation of the relationship leaves the reader not quite sure where their sympathies lie.

Bullet points

- The opening suggests that the two women, although drinking tea together, had little to say and were both just watching the road.
- The social difference between them seems to cause resentment on both sides: the fat woman resents the fact that the thin woman's son has become her son's superior because he was university educated.
- The thin woman resents the fact that there is jealousy about her son's position and no understanding of the sacrifices she made to bring it about.
- They come together in the face of the fear caused by the elder's telegram and show sympathy and understanding of each other: 'She felt the arm of the thin woman around her shoulders.'
- The fat woman suppresses her joy and relief that it's not her son, because she feels it must be the thin woman's son, and it would be wrong.
- When the crisis is passed the two women part without acknowledging that anything unusual had happened between them.

In this 10-mark question, there are up to 2 marks available for part A, up to 2 marks for part B and up to 6 marks for part C. You could gain these by making six basic points, three detailed/ insightful points, or a combination of these. You have to select relevant references and link them to the idea of uneasy relationships.

Hints & tips ★

You are expected to be able to quote from or refer to relevant parts of the short story:
- *'They drank their tea in silence turning away from each other'*
- *'Perhaps he was going in search of his son'*

Or, make reference to scenes and incidents without actually quoting:
- *The fat woman suppresses the desire to dance when she realises it's not her son.*
- *The incident where the two women share sympathy with each other.*

Exercise 4 ✎

Try to make a relevant comment on each of the phrases in the answer to question 3 on page 111. There are six examples (one has already been done for you – see pages 111–12 for simple and developed versions of this example).

Novel

There are **three** kinds of final 10-mark questions:
1. One kind is concerned with identifying a **common theme or central concern**.
2. The second kind is concerned with the use of a **similar technique or set of techniques**.
3. The third kind comments on **character or relationships** (often in combination with a theme or central concern.

Here, the 10-mark question on *Dr Jekyll and Mr Hyde* concentrates on character.

The 10-mark question on *The Cone-Gatherers* concentrates on character and theme.

The 10-mark question on *Sunset Song* concentrates on character.

(A) *Dr Jekyll and Mr Hyde* (extract)

It was late in the afternoon, when Mr Utterson found his way to Dr Jekyll's door, where he was at once admitted by Poole, and carried down by the kitchen offices and across a yard which had once been a garden, to the building which was indifferently
5 known as the laboratory or dissecting rooms. The doctor had bought the house from the heirs of a celebrated surgeon; and his own tastes being rather chemical than anatomical, had changed the destination of the block at the bottom of the garden. It was the first time that the lawyer had been received in that part of his
10 friend's quarters; and he eyed the dingy, windowless structure with curiosity, and gazed round with a distasteful sense of strangeness as he crossed the theatre, once crowded with eager students and now lying gaunt and silent, the tables laden with chemical apparatus, the floor strewn with crates and littered with packing
15 straw, and the light falling dimly through the foggy cupola. At the further end, a flight of stairs mounted to a door covered with red baize; and through this, Mr Utterson was at last received into the doctor's cabinet. It was a large room fitted round with glass presses, furnished, among other things, with a cheval glass and
20 a business table, and looking out upon the court by three dusty windows barred with iron. The fire burned in the grate; a lamp was set lighted on the chimney shelf, for even in the houses the fog began to lie thickly; and there, close up to the warmth, sat Dr Jekyll, looking deathly sick. He did not rise to meet his visitor, but
25 held out a cold hand and bade him welcome in a changed voice.

'And now,' said Mr Utterson, as soon as Poole had left them, 'you have heard the news?'

The doctor shuddered. 'They were crying it in the square,' he said. 'I heard them in my dining-room.'

30 'One word,' said the lawyer. 'Carew was my client, but so are you, and I want to know what I am doing. You have not been mad enough to hide this fellow?'

'Utterson, I swear to God,' cried the doctor, 'I swear to God I will never set eyes on him again. I bind my honour to you that I am
35 done with him in this world. It is all at an end. And indeed he does not want my help; you do not know him as I do; he is safe, he is quite safe; mark my words, he will never more be heard of.'

The lawyer listened gloomily; he did not like his friend's feverish manner. 'You seem pretty sure of him,' said he; 'and for your sake, I
40 hope you may be right. If it came to a trial, your name might appear.'

⇨

⇨

'I am quite sure of him,' replied Jekyll; 'I have grounds for certainty that I cannot share with any one. But there is one thing on which you may advise me. I have – I have received a letter; and I am at a loss whether I should show it to the police. I should like
45 to leave it in your hands, Utterson; you would judge wisely, I am sure; I have so great a trust in you.'

'You fear, I suppose, that it might lead to his detection?' asked the lawyer.

'No,' said the other. 'I cannot say that I care what becomes
50 of Hyde; I am quite done with him. I was thinking of my own character, which this hateful business has rather exposed.'

Utterson ruminated awhile; he was surprised at his friend's selfishness, and yet relieved by it. 'Well,' said he, at last, 'let me see the letter.'

55 The letter was written in an odd, upright hand and signed 'Edward Hyde': and it signified, briefly enough, that the writer's benefactor, Dr Jekyll, whom he had long so unworthily repaid for a thousand generosities, need labour under no alarm for his safety, as he had means of escape on which he placed a sure
60 dependence. The lawyer liked this letter well enough; it put a better colour on the intimacy than he had looked for, and he blamed himself for some of his past suspicions.

'Have you the envelope?' he asked.

'I burned it,' replied Jekyll, 'before I thought what I was about. But
65 it bore no postmark. The note was handed in.'

'Shall I keep this and sleep on it?' asked Utterson.

'I wish you to judge for me entirely,' was the reply. 'I have lost confidence in myself.'

'Well, I shall consider,' returned the lawyer. 'And now one word
70 more: it was Hyde who dictated the terms in your will about that disappearance?'

The doctor seemed seized with a qualm of faintness; he shut his mouth tight and nodded.

'I knew it,' said Utterson. 'He meant to murder you. You had a
75 fine escape.'

'I have had what is far more to the purpose,' returned the doctor solemnly: 'I have had a lesson – O God, Utterson, what a lesson I have had!' And he covered his face for a moment with his hands.

On his way out, the lawyer stopped and had a word or two with
80 Poole. 'By the bye,' said he, 'there was a letter handed in today: what was the messenger like?' But Poole was positive that nothing had come except by post; 'and only circulars by that,' he added.

Robert Louis Stevenson

Questions ❓

1 Read lines 1– 25. Analyse how Stevenson creates an appropriate atmosphere for this meeting between Dr Jekyll and Mr Utterson. You should refer to **at least two** examples. **(4)**
2 Analyse how the language of lines 28–40 shows that Dr Jekyll is in a highly nervous state. **(2)**
3 By looking at the dialogue from lines 63–78, explain how Stevenson emphasises the contrast between the two characters. **(4)**
4 Discuss how Utterson's character contributes to his ability to gather information about the riddle of Dr Jekyll's behaviour, both in this extract and in the novel as a whole. **(10)**

Answers

This section takes you through possible answers to these questions. Remember, though, that there will be many other equally acceptable answers.

1 **Read lines 1–25. Analyse how Stevenson creates an appropriate atmosphere for this meeting between Dr Jekyll and Mr Utterson. You should refer to at least two examples. (4)**
- 'dingy, windowless structure'
- 'distasteful sense of strangeness'
- 'lying gaunt and silent'
- 'littered (with packing straw)'
- 'light falling dimly'
- 'foggy cupola'
- 'three dusty windows barred with iron'
- 'the fog began to lie thickly'
- 'deathly sick'
- 'cold hand'

You are being offered four marks in this question, and you must deal with at least two examples. So you have the choice of dealing with four examples in a basic way or you could deal with fewer in more depth. Any two of the above, when linked with the atmosphere created, could gain up to 2 marks each. There are other comments that could be made about sentence structure and contrast which would be equally valid.

2 **Analyse how the language of lines 28–40 shows that Dr Jekyll is in a highly nervous state. (2)**
- 'the doctor shuddered'
- 'cried the doctor'
- repetition of 'I swear to God' or 'he is safe'
- '(his friend's) feverish manner'

3 **By looking at the dialogue from lines 63–78, explain how Stevenson emphasises the contrast between the two characters. (4)**
The lawyer remains decisive and business-like, asking purposeful questions:
- 'Have you the envelope?' showing his practical desire to know where it came from.
- 'Shall I keep this and sleep on it?' seems the next sensible step to avoid embarrassment for Jekyll.
- 'I knew it' proving to himself that his logical deductions are well-founded.

In contrast, Dr Jekyll betrays agitation:
- 'I have lost confidence in myself' showing his emotional state – 'qualm of faintness'.
- Unable to answer – 'shut his mouth tight and nodded'.

⇨

- Exclamation – 'Oh God ... lesson I have had'.
- Distress shown by 'covered his face with his hands'.

You should deal with each side of the contrast. Each point above would gain 1 mark, with a total of 2 marks available on either 'side'.

4 **Discuss how Utterson's character contributes to his ability to gather information about the riddle of Dr Jekyll's behaviour, both in this extract and in the novel as a whole. (10)**

*To make sure you answer all parts of this question you must do **three** things:*

A *You should be looking at Utterson's characterisation here and throughout the novel.*

B *By referring to this extract, you should look at his characterisation as demonstrated here.*

C *You should show how Utterson's characteristics are consistently displayed throughout the novel and their effect on his relationships with the other characters.*

For example:

A Utterson's characteristic behaviour is to display patience and persistence in dealing with the troubles of his friends, such as his determination to investigate Jekyll's secret. (1) His loyalty is also tested and found to be impregnable in the face of temptation to betray confidences, such as such as when he obeys Lanyon's instruction about the letter. (1)

B In this chapter, Utterson prises information out of Jekyll by careful and sensitive questioning – necessary because of the highly nervous state Jekyll is in after the murder of Carew. Jekyll's declaration 'I am quite done with him' seems to satisfy Utterson at that moment, but his persistence in questioning Poole about the letter raises suspicion again.

C *You should comment on Utterson's qualities which allow him to become the lynchpin of the novel as a whole, as the receiver of the confidences of many informants. You can answer this question either by bullet points or by use of a series of linked statements. You may find that the bullet point method helps you to structure your answer more clearly, or you may find that linked statements allow you to incorporate your comments more easily. You should use which ever method works for you. Both methods are shown below.*

Series of linked statements

Throughout the novel Utterson is important because his trustworthy character means that he retains the confidence of the other characters and thus is given much confidential information. Enfield is reluctant – 'Here is another lesson, to say nothing' – and only with the encouragement of Utterson, relates the story of Hyde's treatment of the little girl.

Utterson's patience in pursuit of Hyde gives us a glimpse into the distress of Hyde/Jekyll when Hyde/Jekyll is mentioned, showing the reader some sort of perilous relationship between the two. Utterson's questioning in the three interviews he has with Jekyll allows him to learn more through Jekyll's distress.

His dependability makes him the natural receiver of Lanyon's letter, 'for the hand of J.G. Utterson ALONE', which contains the real answer to the riddle.

Poole also chooses Utterson to run to in distress at the turn events have taken in the laboratory. Finally, Jekyll's trust in Utterson is sealed by making him the beneficiary of his Will.

Bullet points

- Utterson's trustworthiness gets information about Hyde from Enfield about the trampling of the little girl.
- In his interviews with Jekyll, he manages to get Jekyll to confide, at least partially, in him.
- Dr Lanyon chooses Utterson as the person he should tell about Jekyll's experiment.

- Utterson's integrity doesn't allow him to read the letter before it's too late, but this too is a part of Utterson's steady character.
- Poole also trusts Utterson when his master appears to be in an impossible position.
- Jekyll, finally, shows his appreciation of Utterson's qualities by naming him as his beneficiary in the Will.

In this 10-mark question, there are up to 2 marks available for part A, up to 2 marks for part B and up to 6 marks for part C. You could gain these by making six basic points, three detailed/insightful points, or a combination of these. You have to select relevant references and link them to Utterson's character.

Hints & tips

As in the short story question that precedes this, you are expected to be able to quote from, or refer to, other relevant parts of the novel:
- *'professional honour and faith to his dead friend were stringent obligations'*

Or, you can make reference to scenes and incidents without quoting directly:
- *Enfield recounts the incident of the little girl to Utterson.*

Hints & tips

You will notice that the first three questions are very like the questions asked about the short story. When thinking about answers to prose questions you can gain a lot from your understanding of similar questions in the Analysis section of Chapter 3 (pages 50–71).

(B) *The Cone-Gatherers* (extract)

Hidden among the spruces at the edge of the ride, near enough to catch the smell of larch off the cones and to be struck by some of those thrown, stood Duror the gamekeeper, in an icy sweat of hatred, with his gun aimed all the time at the feebleminded
5   hunchback grovelling over the rabbit. To pull the trigger, requiring far less force than to break a rabbit's neck, and then to hear simultaneously the clean report of the gun and the last obscene squeal of the killed dwarf would have been for him, he thought, release too, from the noose of disgust and despair drawn, these
10 past few days, so much tighter.

Hints & tips

*Remember that references can be to actions and incidents, or in the form of quotation. You may find it easier to refer to actions and incidents in longer texts, such as a novel, and to use quotations more freely in answers on poetry. It is entirely up to you. But you **must** make reference to the text in some form in your answers.*

He had waited for over an hour there to see them pass. Every minute
had been a purgatory of humiliation: it was as if he was in their
service, forced to wait upon his masters. Yet he hated and despised
them far more powerfully than he ever had liked and respected
15 Sir Colin and Lady Runcie-Campbell. While waiting, he had imagined
them in the darkness missing their footing in the tall tree and
coming crashing down through the sea of branches to lie dead on
the ground. So passionate had been his visualising of that scene, he
seemed himself to be standing on the floor of a fantastic sea, with an
20 owl and a herd of roe-deer flitting by quiet as fish, while the yellow
ferns and bronzen brackens at his feet gleamed like seaweed, and
the spruce trees swayed above him like submarine monsters.

He could have named, item by item, leaf and fruit and branch, the
overspreading tree of revulsion in him; but he could not tell the force
25 which made it grow, any more than he could have explained the life
in himself, or in the dying rabbit, or in any of the trees about him.

This wood had always been his stronghold and sanctuary; there
were many places secret to him where he had been able to fortify
his sanity and hope. But now the wood was invaded and defiled; its
30 cleansing and reviving virtues were gone. Into it had crept
this hunchback, himself one of nature's freaks, whose abject
acceptance of nature, like the whining protestations of a heathen in
front of an idol, had made acceptance no longer possible for Duror
himself. He was humpbacked, with one shoulder higher than the
35 other; he had no neck, and on the mis-shapen lump of his body sat a
face so beautiful and guileless as to be a diabolical joke. He was now
in the wood, protected, not to be driven out or shot at or trapped or
trampled on; and with him was his brother, tall, thin, grey-haired,
with an appearance of harsh meditation obviously false in a man
40 who read no books and could only spell through a newspaper word
by word: They had been brought into the wood: a greasy shed, hardly
bigger than a rabbit-hutch, had been knocked together in a couple
of hours, and set up in one of Duror's haunts, a clearing amongst
cypresses, where, in early summer, hyacinths had bloomed in thou-
45 sands. Already, after only a week, the ground round about was filthy
with their refuse and ordure. They were to be allowed to pollute
every tree in the wood except the silver firs near the big house.

Duror was alone in his obsession. No one else found their presence
obnoxious; everybody accepted the forester's description of them
50 as shy, honest, hard-working, respectable men …

Robin Jenkins

Hints & tips

*If you have a choice
between this Scottish text
and another, you should
look carefully at **all** the
questions asked on **this**
novel. You may be quite
happy with the choice of
The Cone-Gatherers but
always look at the last
question (in this case,
question 4) to see what it
is you have been asked to
do in the context of the
novel as a whole. Before
you make up your mind
finally, you should **always**
have looked at Section 2
before making your choice.*

Exercise 5 🖉

The first three questions are very similar to the type of questions
already dealt with in the short story section. You could attempt to
answer these even though you have not studied this novel in your
course. The ability to understand and analyse a short passage of fiction
cannot be practised too often.

(Answers on page 131)

Questions ?

1 By referring closely to at least two examples in lines 1–10, analyse how Jenkins conveys Duror's feelings towards Calum. **(4)**

2 In lines 11–18 analyse how Jenkins creates a sense of the length of time that Duror has been waiting. **(2)**

3 By referring to at least two examples from lines 27–50, analyse how the writer shows Duror's disgust as to the change which has happened in his wood. **(4)**

4 Referring to this extract and to elsewhere in the novel, discuss how Jenkins explores Duror's obsessive nature. **(10)**

Answer

This section takes you through a possible answer to question 4. Remember, though, that there will be many other equally acceptable answers.

4 **Referring to this extract and to elsewhere in the novel, discuss how Jenkins explores Duror's obsessive nature. (10)**

*To make sure you answer all the parts of this last question you must do **three** things:*

A *You should show how your understanding of obsession has been developed.*

B *Next you should show how the idea of 'obsession' has been dealt with in the extract in front of you.*

C *Then you must show, by referring to the rest of the novel, how the idea of Duror's obsession is explored.*

For example:

A Duror's obsessive nature is presented as being dangerous, both to himself and others (1) and destroys his ability to act rationally and observe the normal terms of morality, as at the deer drive where he is seen to be out of control. (1)

B The reference to his waiting 'for over an hour' just to see them pass, and the idea that he is 'forced' to wait on them as if they were 'his masters' suggests an irrational compulsion to spy on the brothers – in fact, an obsession.

C *You should now show how Duror's obsession is illustrated in incidents throughout the novel. You can answer this question either by bullet points or by use of a series of linked statements. You may find that the bullet point method helps you to structure your answer more clearly, or you may find that linked statements allow you to incorporate your comments more easily. You should use whichever method works for you.*

Bullet points

- Duror's obsession with the cone-gatherers is the most important element of the plot. It leads directly to the final tragedy of two deaths.
- When he sees the light in the brothers' hut, he breaks out into a sweat 'of revulsion'.
- At the deer drive he loses all sense of where he is or what he's doing when he kills the deer. He is 'possessed by a fury' and has to be restrained from attacking Calum.
- In the bar at Lendrick he cannot keep his mind off Calum sitting in the alcove of the pub, and he pays only superficial attention to the conversation he is supposed to be involved in.
- Roderick watches Duror watching the hut obsessively again for a long time and feels the presence of evil, although he does not understand what it is.

- Finally, Duror is compelled to kill Calum after his meeting with Graham in the wood where Duror's powerful fist is 'biting his chest like a gigantic spider' and he moves off 'stalking' towards the trees.
- After killing Calum he seems to have lost his anger but then had to kill himself because he had become so closed off by his obsession that he had to die too.

In this 10-mark question, there are up to 2 marks available for part A, up to 2 marks for part B and up to 6 marks for part C. You could gain these by making six basic points, three detailed/insightful points, or a combination of these. You have to select relevant references and link them to Duror's obsession.

Hints & tips

*Remember that references can be to actions and incidents, or in the form of quotation. You may find it easier to refer to actions and incidents in longer texts, such as a novel, and to use quotations more freely in answers on poetry. It is entirely up to you. But you **must** make reference to the text in some form in your answers.*

(C) *Sunset Song*
(extract from 'Prelude')

But Rob of the Mill had never a thought of what Kinraddie said of him. Further along the Kinraddie road it stood, the Mill, on the corner of the side-road that led up to Upperhill, and for ten years now had Rob bided there alone, managing the
5   Mill and reading the books of a coarse creature Ingersoll that made watches and didn't believe in God. He'd aye two–three fine pigs about the Mill had Rob, and fine might well they be for what did he feed them on but bits of corn and barley he'd nicked out of the sacks folk brought him to the Mill to grind?
10   Nor could a body deny but that Long Rob's boar was one of the best in the Mearns; and they'd bring their sows from far afield as Laurencekirk to have them set by that boar of his, a meikle, pretty brute of a beast.

Forbye the Mill and his swine and hens Rob had a Clydesdale and
15   a sholtie beast he ploughed his twenty acres with, and a cow or so that never calved, for he'd never time to send them to the bull though well might he have taken the time instead of sweating and chaving like a daft one to tear up the coarse moorland behind the Mill and turn it into a park. He'd started that three years before
20   and wasn't half through with it yet, it was filled with great holes and ponds and choked with meikle broom-roots thick as the arm of a man, you never saw a dafter ploy. They'd hear Rob out in that coarse ground hard at work when they went to bed, the rest of Kinraddie, whistling away to himself as though it were nine
25   o'clock in the forenoon and the sun shining bravely. He'd whistle *Ladies of Spain* and *There was a young maiden* and *The lass that made the bed for me*, but devil the lass he'd ever taken to his bed, and maybe that was as well for the lass; she'd have seen feint the much of him in it beside her.

Hints & tips

*If you have a choice between this Scottish text and another, you should look carefully at **all** the questions asked on **this** novel. You may be quite happy with the choice of Sunset Song but always look at the last question (in this case question 4) to see what it is you have been asked to do in the context of the novel as a whole. Before you make up your mind finally, you should **always** have looked at Section 2 before making your choice.*

30 For after a night of it like that he'd be out again at the keek of
    day, and sometimes he'd have the Clydesdale or the sholtie out
    there with him and they'd be fine friends, the three of them, till
    the beasts would move off when he didn't want them or wouldn't
    move when he did; and then he'd fair go mad with them and call
35 them all the coarsest names he could lay tongue to till you'd think
    he'd be heard over half the Mearns; and he'd leather the horses till
    folk spoke of sending for the Cruelty, though he'd a way with the
    beasts too, and would be friends with them again in a minute, and
    when he'd been away at the smithy in Drumlithie or the joiner's in
40 Arbuthnott they'd come running from the other end of the parks
    at the sight of him and he'd get off his bicycle and feed them with
    lumps of sugar he bought and carried about with him.

    He thought himself a gey man with horses, did Rob, and God! he'd
    tell you stories about horses till you'd fair be grey in the head,
45 but he never wearied of them himself, the long, rangy childe.
    Long he was, with small bones maybe but gey broad for all that,
    with a small head on him and a thin nose and eyes smoky blue
    as an iron coulter on a winter morning, aye glinting, and a long
    mouser the colour of ripe corn it was, hanging down the sides
50 of his mouth so that the old minister had told him he looked like
    a Viking and he'd said *Ah well, minister, as long as I don't look
    like a parson I'll wrestle through the world right content*, and the
    minister said he was a fool and godless, and his laughter like
    thorns crackling under a pot. And Rob said he'd rather be a thorn
55 than a sucker any day, for he didn't believe in ministers or kirks,
    he'd learned that from the books of Ingersoll though God knows
    if the creature's logic was as poor as his watches he was but a
    sorry prop to lean on. But Rob said he was fine, and if Christ came
    down to Kinraddie he'd be welcome enough to a bit of meal or
60 milk at the Mill, but damn the thing he'd get at the Manse. So that
    was Long Rob and the stir at the Mill, some said he wasn't all
    there but others said Ay, that he was, and a bit over.

    Lewis Grassic Gibbon

Questions

1   Read lines 1–6. Explain how Gibbon quickly gives us an impression of
    Rob's personality. **(2)**
2   Analyse how the language in lines 14–22 emphasises the sheer hard work
    Rob undertakes. You should refer to **at least two** examples. **(4)**
3   Read lines 46–60. By referring to **at least two** examples, analyse the
    language Gibbon uses to highlight the difference of opinion between
    Rob and the minister. **(4)**
4   By referring to this extract and to the novel as a whole, discuss how the
    idea of Rob's individualism is developed. **(10)**

Answers

This section takes you through possible answers to these questions. Remember, though, that there will be many other equally acceptable answers.

1 **Read lines 1–6. Explain how Gibbon quickly gives us an impression of Rob's personality. (2)**
   - The opening sentence 'never a thought of what Kinraddie said' immediately suggests that the character is an individualist – his own man.
   - He is shown to be an atheist as he read books by someone who 'didn't believe in God'.
   - In the society of the time this would be seen as totally unacceptable/revolutionary.

2 **Analyse how the language in lines 14–22 emphasises the sheer hard work Rob undertakes. You should refer to at least two examples. (4)**
   - 'sweating and chaving (like a daft one)'
   - 'tear up (the coarse moorland)'
   - 'filled with great holes and ponds'
   - 'choked (with meikle broom-roots)'
   - 'thick as the arm of a man'

   You are being offered 4 marks in this question, and you must deal with at least two examples. So, you have the choice of dealing with four examples in a basic way or you could deal with fewer in more depth.

3 **Read lines 46–60. By referring to at least two examples, analyse the language Gibbon uses to highlight the difference of opinion between Rob and the minister. (4)**
   - 'told him he looked like a Viking'
   - 'said he was a fool and godless'
   - 'laughter like thorns crackling under a pot'
   - 'rather be a thorn than a sucker'
   - 'Christ (would) be welcome … at the Mill'
   - 'but damn the thing he'd get at the Manse'

   The answers might include the pagan connotations of 'Viking'; the linking of 'fool' and 'godless'; the simile about laughter; the use of contrast between the Mill and the Manse. You are being offered four marks in this question, and you must deal with at least two examples. So, you have the choice of dealing with four examples in a basic way or you could deal with fewer in more depth.

4 **By referring to this extract and to the novel as a whole, discuss how the idea of Rob's individualism is developed. (10)**
   Your answer here has to cover the three aspects that you are now familiar with:

   A *Rob refuses to conform to the cultural norms of society if he does not believe in them, even when under enormous pressure to do so. (1) His rejection of patriotism and the accepted attitude to the war leaves him isolated, socially and economically in the community, for example when farmers stop trading with him. (1)*

   B *How this is identified in the extract you have just read, including reference to:*
   - *the fact that he had 'never a thought of what Kinraddie said'*
   - *the fact that he 'bided there alone' seemingly needing no other companion*
   - *his continuing to fight to improve his land in the face of the attitude summed up by 'you never saw a dafter ploy'*
   - *his atheism – 'he didn't believe in ministers or the kirk'*
   - *his quarrel with the minister – 'rather be a thorn than a sucker'.*

   C *You can answer this question either by bullet points or by use of a series of linked statements. You may find that the bullet point method helps you to structure your answer more clearly, or you*

⇒

⇨ *may find that linked statements allow you to incorporate your comment more easily. You should use whichever method works for you. Both of these methods are shown below.*

Series of linked statements

The introduction to Rob clearly states that he had 'never a thought of what Kinraddie said about him'. This is shown in his discussions on politics and education with Chae and others at the threshing; and his antipathy to the Kirk is illustrated throughout in his quarrel with Gibbon, the minister, whose sermon caused Rob to be hounded by a mob because Gibbon had called him 'pro German'. Even when Rob refuses to be conscripted, and knows that the punishment will be imprisonment, he lets himself be carried away to prison rather than give up his principles. His hunger strike eventually leads to his release, physically broken: 'He took the arm of the first one … at snail's pace'. He survives even when he is released into a hostile community where only Chris will speak to him and help him, and manages to be true to himself.

His decision to enlist finally, when he was no longer being forced into it, seems to be driven by the idea that he owed it to his fellow men to die beside them even though he still thought that 'all the world had gone daft' and his bravery in the last days of the war is just another version of his individuality.

Bullet points

- Rob's discussions with Chae and others on the subject of politics and education show his strong views.
- His defence of himself in discussions about his attitude to the war.
- His stubbornness even after the sermon brought a mob to his door.
- His return from prison and his endurance of the hostility and cold shoulder of the community.
- His paradoxical decision finally to join up, and his motives for doing so.

Two of these references well-explained in the context of the question, or three commented on more simply could provide a sufficient answer.

Hints & tips

*Remember that references can be to actions and incidents, or in the form of quotation. You may find it easier to refer to actions and incidents in longer texts, such as a novel, and to use quotations more freely in answers on poetry. It is entirely up to you. But you **must** make reference to the text in some form in your answers.*

Drama

There are **three** kinds of final 10-mark questions:

1. One kind is concerned with identifying a **common theme or central concern**.
2. The second kind is concerned with the use of a **similar technique or set of techniques**.
3. The third kind comments on **character or relationships** (often in combination with a theme or central concern).

The 10-mark question on *The Cheviot, the Stag and the Black, Black Oil* concentrates on techniques. The text of the following play is interesting as it was built in a collaborative way by its first cast and the writer, John McGrath. It was subject to change depending on the venue and the audience. Not all of the play was performed every time, and sometimes the script varied, but the original intention of opening the eyes of Scottish people to the exploitation they had suffered over centuries remained the same.

The Cheviot, the Stag and the Black, Black Oil (extract)

Author's note: I was present at the second ever performance of this play at the Macrobert Arts Centre in Stirling. When the play finished, the actors talked to the audience about the play. A very old man stood up at the back and said, 'My mother told me that when she was four years old, she remembered being carried up the side of the glen in her mother's arms and watching her house burning. She told me, "You might forgive, son, but never forget."' You can imagine the electrifying effect that had on the cast and the audience.

Ghillie whistles up the Beaters

Ghillie: Any moment now sir …

Lord Crask: Here come the grouse, Lady Phosphate –

Lady Ph: What?

5 **Lord Crask:** The grouse –

Lady Ph: Oh, how lovely – *(She gets out a sten gun.)* I find it so moving that all over the north of North Britain, healthy, vigorous people are deriving so much innocent pleasure at so little cost to their fellow human beings.

10 *Barrage. Ghillie aims Lord Crask's gun up higher, struggles with him. Lady Phosphate fires her sten from the hip. Bombs, shells, etc. Barrage ends.*

Ghillie: Oh no – Thon was a nice wee boy.

Music – guitar and mandolin begins. Lord Crask and Lady
15 *Phosphate sing a duet.*

Both: Oh it's awfully, frightfully, ni-i-ice,

Shooting stags, my dear, and grice –

And there's nothing quite so righ-it-it

As a fortnight catching trite:

20 And if the locals should complain,

Well we can clear them off again. ⇨

⇨ **Lady Ph:** We'll clear the straths

Lord Crask: We'll clear the paths

Lady Ph: We'll clear the bens

25 **Lord Crask:** We'll clear the glens

Both: We'll show them we're the ruling class.

Repeat from: 'We'll clear the straths'. Instrumental half verse.

Lord Crask *(Speaking over the music)*: Oh they all come here, you know – Lady Phosphate of Runcorn – her husband's big in

30 chemicals – she has a great interest in Highland culture.

Lady Ph: How I wish that I could paint –

For the people are so quaint

I said so at our ceilidh

To dear Benjamin Disraeli.

35 Mr Landseer showed the way –

He gets commissions every day –

The Silvery Tay.

Lord Crask: The Stag at Bay

Lady Ph: The misty moor –

40 **Lord Crask:** Sir George McClure

Both: We are the Monarchs of the Glen –

Lady Ph: The Shepherd Boy

Lord Crask: Old Man of Hoy

Lady Ph: And Fingal's Cave

45 **Lord Crask:** The Chieftain Brave

Both: We are Monarchs of the Glen

Lord Crask: We love to dress as Highland lads

In our tartans, kilts and plaids –

Lady Ph: And to dance the shean trew-oo-oos

50 In our bonnie, ghillie, shoes –

Both: And the skirling of the pi-broch

As it echoes o'er the wee-loch

Lord Crask: We love the games

Lady Ph: Their funny names

⇨

⇒

55 **Lord Crask**: The sporran's swing

Lady Ph: The Highland fling

Both: We are more Scottish than the Scotch.

Lady Ph: The Camera-ha

Lord Crask: The Slainte-Vah

60 **Lady Ph:** Is that the lot?

Both: Sir Walter Scott –

We are more Scottish than the Scotch.

They become more serious. They turn their guns on the audience.

Lord Crask: But although we think you're quaint,

65 Don't forget to pay your rent,

And if you should want your land,

We'll cut off your grasping hand.

Lady Ph: You had better learn your place,

You're a low and servile race –

70 We've cleared the straths

Lord Crask: We've cleared the paths

Lady Ph: We've cleared the bens

Lady Ph: We've cleared the glens

Both: And we can do it once again –

75 **Lady Ph**: We've got the brass

Lord Crask: We've got the class

Lady Ph: We've got the law

Both: We need no more –

We'll show you we're the ruling class.

Song ends.

John McGrath

Questions

1 Identify one action and one phrase from lines 6–13 ('Oh how lovely … nice wee boy') and show how they display a careless or patronising attitude to the Highlands and the Highlanders. **(2)**

2 'She has a great interest in Highland culture' (line 30). Analyse the language used by Lady Phosphate and Lord Crask in the song from lines 31–62, showing how it actually demeans Scottish culture rather than celebrates it. You should refer to at least two examples. **(4)**

3 Analyse the language used about the Scots after the stage direction in line 63, showing how it marks a turning point in attitude. You should refer to at least two examples. **(4)**

4 The use of music and/or song in this play is significant. By referring to this extract and elsewhere in the play, discuss the effect of these elements. **(10)**

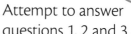

Exercise 6

Attempt to answer questions 1, 2 and 3.

This is very difficult without having studied the play, because so much of its power depends on the 'performance' elements of the drama. But you could give it a go.

(Answers on page 131.)

Answer

This section takes you through a possible answer to question 4. Remember, though, that there will be many other equally acceptable answers.

4 **The use of music and/or song in this play is significant. By referring to this extract and elsewhere in the play, discuss the effect of these elements. (10)**
   *To make sure you answer all the parts of this last question you must do **three** things:*
   A *You should show your understanding of the significance and impact of music in theatrical performance.*
   B *Next you should show how the contribution of the music in the extract in front of you is successful.*
   C *For the 6 additional marks available you need to refer to the success of music and song elsewhere in the play.*

   For example:
   A The power of music and song allows the emotions of an audience, such as sadness or outrage to be affected by more than just the words of the drama. (1) It can set atmosphere and create changes of pace and mood to underpin the 'message' of the play. (1)
   B The use of the song here allows the use of rhyme and repetition initially to mock the attitudes and accents of the English aristocrats – 'grice' and 'trice' for example instead of 'grouse' and 'trout'. The repetition of chorus lines helps to make the sentiments clearer – for example, 'we'll clear the paths', etc. and 'we're the ruling class'.
   C *You would be expected to make several references to the use of music and/or song elsewhere in the play. The following illustrates an answer using bullet points, although you could answer it in a series of linked statements if that is your preferred method of working.*

Bullet points

- Important ideas are transmitted through the emotional atmosphere created by the music.
- Throughout the play song is used to create emotion in the audience. The opening of the play has Scottish fiddle music playing as the audience comes in to establish the scene in a Scottish cultural setting.
- The song used in the section of the play describing the opposition to the Clearances ('The Battle of the Braes') literally gives a voice to the Highlanders, and the repetition of the chorus:
  'Oh the battle was long but the people were strong
  You should have been there that day'
  brings the audience (who are encouraged to sing along) emotionally onside with the actors.
- The use of Gaelic songs, even though only a small proportion of the audience understands the words, is evocative of a bygone age and the dying culture of the Gaels, which was speeded by the oppression of Scottish customs such as wearing tartan, using English as the only medium of education and suppressing the language altogether. In this case, the music carries the meaning, which the words spoken would not.
- The final song, which is in Gaelic, is sung, then translated into English for the audience and then sung again to provide a climax to the play.

In this 10-mark question, there are up to 2 marks available for part A, up to 2 marks for part B and up to 6 marks for part C. You could gain these by making six basic points, three detailed/insightful points, or a combination of these. You have to select relevant references and link them to the effect of music and/or song.

Answers

Exercise 1 (page 102)

- 'own country' suggests a sense of belonging being taken away from her, creating a sense of abandonment.
- 'fell through the fields' suggests lack of control and speed of the experience, creating a helpless feeling as if the ground were falling away from the train.
- 'the miles rushed back' – the personification of the miles suggests that each mile of distance is running away from her back to her home where she can't follow them, as if they (the miles) don't like where she is going to either.
- 'the city, the street, the house, the vacant rooms' – the climax of this series. The smallest space she is leaving is left till last, which shows how her memory of the home she is leaving is becoming concentrated on the rooms in the house where up until now she has been happy.
- 'stared' suggests that she is unhappily fixing her eyes on the only familiar object she has left.
- 'blind toy' – the fact that the toy is blind makes it seem a sad sight, or because it is blind it doesn't see what she sees – a bleak future.
- 'holding its paw' suggests that the poet is trying to gain some comfort from the touch of an old familiar object.

Exercise 2 (page 103)

- Imagery: 'All childhood is an emigration' suggests that children are uncertain enough about the world around them and how it changes without the added stress of changing homes.
- Word choice:
  - 'resigned' suggests a kind of helplessness on the part of the child.
  - 'unimagined' suggests a kind of unfamiliarity with the district, the unknown exists round every corner.
  - 'big boys eating worms' – the shocking nature of their behaviour makes the child feel different and possibly threatened by a sort of mindless cruelty.
  - 'don't understand' suggests that the inability of the child to understand a new accent/dialect further increases her fear of the unknown.
  - Contrast: 'some are slow'/'others are sudden' shows that no matter the circumstances, the feeling of displacement can happen in a wide variety of situations and you can't predict when – causing anxiety.
  - The use of direct speech: the child's voice with the very simple words betray a sense of loss and discomfort.

Exercise 3 (page 106)

1.
  - 'unwind' – connotations of becoming looser, more expansive, less uptight, contributes to a contented, carefree atmosphere/mood.
  - 'The kitchen filled with the smell of itself' – this image/personification suggests that the kitchen is somehow contented with what it is achieving although, of course, it is Mrs Midas who is actually doing the cooking.
  - 'relaxed' – connotations of stillness, lack of tension, also contribute to the contented mood.
  - 'steamy breath' is a continuation of the kitchen image, possibly suggesting sighing in contentment, enveloping the kitchen in a comfort blanket – a mood of well-being and calm.
  - 'gently' suggests that nothing sudden or harsh can happen – all movement is quiet and calm, suggesting contentment.

⇨

- the sequence 'So … then … ' seems quite unrushed – nothing bad seems about to happen (it would be possible to say exactly the opposite about 'So … then' saying that it leads up to something dramatic).

You would not be required to cover all of these examples. Two would be enough.

2
- 'So … then' seems likely to lead up to something dramatic.
- Imagery: 'spitting out the teeth of the rich' is the first indication that things are going wrong. The corn is being compared to gold teeth, too hard to eat, and therefore inedible.
- Word choice: 'toyed' suggests a childish delight in turning things to gold, progressing from 'his spoon' to all the cutlery on the table – a process that speeds up in a sort of terror.
- Word choice: 'shaking hand' suggests that she is losing control.
- Climax: from 'glass' to 'goblet' to 'golden chalice' shows the unbelievable and relentless process of things turning into gold under her very eyes, leading to her scream.

You are being offered four marks in this question, and you must deal with at least two examples. So, you have the choice of dealing with four examples in a basic way or you could deal with fewer in more depth.

3
- 'I'd just poured a glass of wine' – informal, confidential tone.
- 'So I opened one' – simple statement.
- 'Now' as an introduction to the next part of the poem, carrying the reader into the story.
- 'On.' Single-word sentence conveys her surprise.
- 'I thought to myself'– again, the reader is being allowed to follow her thoughts.
- 'Is he putting fairy lights in the tree? – the self-questioning makes her puzzlement believable.
- 'I said, What in the name of God is going on?' – a natural question in the circumstances, therefore in character.
- 'shaking hand' – betrays her nervousness.
- 'It was then that I started to scream' – it all becomes too much for her, and this statement ends the first part of the story – we want to know what happens next.

Again, you have the choice of dealing with four examples in a basic way or you could deal with fewer in more depth.

Exercise 4 (page 113)

- 'blaring … savagely' effectively gives an impression of the volume of the sound – loud and brassy, and the emotion of the driver being out of control and wanting to inflict harm on someone: a simpler answer might look like this: 'blaring … savagely' gives the impression that the man makes his car make a loud noise because he is feeling violent. (*This comment attempts to deal only with the connotations of 'savagely'.*)
- 'crowded like rats' – the simile is effective in giving the feeling of being hemmed in (in this case by traffic) and a generally claustrophobic atmosphere is suggested; rats have unpleasant associations with disease and aggression and living in crowded city situations.
- 'that didn't used to be here' suggests a sort of nostalgia for what was there, or possibly a hopelessness about what is there.
- 'yellow lights rayed' suggests garish harsh light attacking the darkness.
- 'red globes' suggests that the cafés were perhaps in some way dangerous, or merely garish, as above.
- 'hardly recognise' suggests bewilderment and resentment at the changes.

Exercise 5 (page 119)

1. • 'icy sweat of hatred' suggests the extent of the hate – it is almost like an illness.
   • 'feebleminded hunchback' – both of these imperfections add to Duror's revulsion.
   • 'grovelling' suggests disgust at the scrabbling around uncontrollably.
   • 'obscene squeal' – the revulsion Duror feels is against some gross obscenity that has the capacity to offend.
   • 'noose' suggests that Duror is trapped by his own obsession with Calum, almost to the extent that he can hardly breathe.
   • 'disgust'/'despair' – both of these words sum up his hatred and revulsion at Calum's deformities.

2. • The repetition of 'waited' and 'wait' adds to the sense of time passing.
   • 'over an hour' – when added to the idea of minutes in the next sentence this makes the time seem very long and drawn-out.
   • 'every minute' suggests that each minute has seemed much longer, emphasising the extent of the wait.
   • 'purgatory' in its religious context is the place where people with sins on their conscience had to spend an infinity of time before being admitted to heaven.
   • 'wait upon his masters' has two meanings – not just the time, but the suggestion that he is their servant. This adds to Duror's feeling of endless waiting.

3. • Duror can recognise that his feelings of disgust are growing in him as a tree grows, little by little, in all parts of his mind – the equivalent of the leaf, fruit and branch, reaching all parts of his being.
   • He can't identify why it is growing; he doesn't understand, but feels its power.

Exercise 6 (page 127)

1. • Action: the careless shooting of 'the wee boy'.
   • Phrase: 'the north of North Britain' doesn't even recognise Scotland as a separate country, only a region of Britain.
   or (possibly)
   • The rest of the speech shows little understanding of the realities of Highland life.

2. • 'quaint' suggests subjects/objects to be studied with curiosity/amusement.
   • 'we are the Monarchs of the Glen' – reference to typical 'Highland scenery' pictures.
   • they (the English) are assuming the superior position.
   • 'dress as Highland lads' suggests belittling the Highlanders by perceiving them as young and unimportant.
   • 'bonnie, ghillie, shoes' – ghillie shoes are workwear for Highlanders but demoted to dance duties by the English dancing Highland dances.
   • Rhyme of 'pi-broch' with 'wee-loch' creates humour and thus trivialises the pibroch, which is the term for the 'great music' of Scotland.
   • 'funny names' – trivialises the traditional clan names.
   • Scotch (rather than Scottish), which by the nineteenth century was seen by the Scots as an English word used in a patronising manner.
   Any four of these with a reasonable comment showing how they demean the Scots.

3
- 'grasping' suggests the Scots are greedy in wanting to own their own land (anti-Scots).
- 'low' suggests inferiority.
- 'servile' suggests only fit for a lower level of society.
- 'cleared' – removed the Scots as a hindrance to their (the aristocrats') use of the land, or repetition of 'cleared' suggesting their power to do anything they like.
- 'brass' – the English have the money, not the Scots.
- 'class' – they are 'upper' class and therefore superior to the ordinary Highlander.
- 'law' – they have the forces of the laws of property, etc. on their side.
- 'ruling class' – they have the power, not the Scots.

Any four of these with a reasonable comment showing their superior, non-compromising attitude to their hold on the land and its associated rights.

Section 2: Critical Essay

Section 2 is worth 20 marks, and having completed Section 1 you should have 45 minutes left!

Section 2 requires you to write **one** Critical Essay on a previously studied text from Drama, Prose, Poetry, Film and TV Drama or Language Study. There are two restrictions on what you can and cannot do in the two sections of the exam paper:

● You must not use the same **text** twice.
● Each of your answers must be on a different **genre**.

For example, if you have answered on Scottish poetry in Section 1, you cannot write your critical essay on poetry of any kind, Scottish or from anywhere else in the world.

How you approach your choice in Section 2 will depend on which texts you have been taught and which you have prepared for the exam.

There is some psychological evidence to suggest that if you very quickly scan the questions in Section 2 before getting down to answering Section 1, then some part of your brain might have been working away at clarifying your choice for Section 2 while the 'active' part of your brain has actually been busy answering the questions in Section 1. You might like to try this to see if it works for you. Remember, however, that time is very tight in the Critical Reading paper.

When you have completed your answer to Section 1, you should read **all** the questions in **each** part of Section 2 that apply to you. For example, if you have just completed an answer on *Sunset Song*, and you have studied a play and poems but **not** Film and TV or Language, then you should look at questions 1–3 and 10–12.

Preparation for the Critical Essay questions involves both mastering **essential skills** and acquiring **good knowledge** of your texts.

Essential skills

1 Show knowledge and understanding of the chosen text.
2 Construct a relevant argument.
3 Select evidence to support your argument.
4 Analyse the effect of language/filmic techniques.
5 Engage with the text and the question.
6 Evaluate the effectiveness of the text with respect to the question.
7 Write in a technically accurate way.

If you neglect skill 7, and write an essay that fails to meet the minimum requirements for technical accuracy, then the essay cannot gain more than 9 marks out of 20, no matter how good its content is.

1 Show knowledge and understanding of the chosen text

Knowledge is the first basic requirement – you should know your text thoroughly. There is really no major skill required for that except a bit of memory work and revision.

Knowledge covers aspects of the text such as who the characters are, what happens – the events and where – in which period/society/place/country. For some poems this list may be slightly different, but even there the questions *Who?*, *What?*, *Where?* and *When?* will generally apply.

Understanding requires a bit more skill. The characters and events don't just happen in a vacuum; they will be 'concerned' with some aspect of life. What we call the 'central concerns' or sometimes the 'theme' of the text are those aspects that make literature worth reading. They expand our minds, our sympathies and our emotional capacity. They let us watch, appreciate and learn from the acting out of parts of the human drama in our minds. They give us what is called 'vicarious experience'. We learn how to put ourselves in others' shoes, and learn a little about life and how it is lived outside our own immediate environment/family/society/generation. At the end of your reading you have to be able to answer questions such as *How?* and *Why?*

For example, in a romantic novel the events may describe the ups, downs, misunderstandings and reconciliations of a central couple, but the central concerns could be any of a multitude of suggestions: the effects of the modern work/life balance; the tyranny of psychological dependency within a relationship; the strains of financial inequality between the partners; the liberating of a relationship from the constraints of society; the value of mutual support in adversity… and it is those central concerns that make us value a text.

2 Construct a relevant argument

We have come across the idea of an 'argument' twice already: once when discussing discursive writing in Chapter 1 (page 3) and again on page 34 when working on your reading skills. The concept is exactly the same in Critical Essays.

You have been asked a question about a text and you have to create a convincing series of points that answer that question. The chances are that each point is going to be contained in a paragraph, and that there will be links between these paragraphs that move towards your conclusion. For the purposes of exemplification, we will use the following synopsis of a rather limited imaginary novel.

Hints & tips

The SQA's definition of technical accuracy for the Critical Essay is:
few errors in spelling, grammar, sentence construction, punctuation and paragraphing and the ability to be understood at first reading.
If minimum standards are not achieved the maximum mark which can be awarded is 9.

The Tale of X and Y

Character X lives in a cottage several miles from a small village. He is generally unsociable – he does not invite anyone to his house. He is regarded in the village as a bit eccentric – he roams the countryside at night surrounded by his dogs, but is never seen outside during the day. The people of the village are therefore inclined to make up rumours about his past life. His family has disowned him because he is supposed to have been the reason for the loss of some family property. This is not entirely true – the property was conned out of him by character Y as part of a scam investment scheme. X had hoped to help his youngest sister to start a new life in Canada. He is hiding her mistakes from the rest of the family, but can be pressured by Y who knows the whole story. Y has lied to X's family in order to keep him from being reunited with them. Y has to keep the family 'sweet' because he wants to marry into the family and gain control of their business, which is in opposition to his.

Example 1

With this imaginary novel in mind, look at the following question.

⑦ Question

- Choose a novel in which a main character is isolated from his or her society. Explain the reasons for this isolation and discuss to what extent the character's personality and actions are responsible for it.

The argument could look something like this:

Character X is isolated – give examples of his isolation – lack of friends – remote house, etc.

The writer establishes reasons for isolation:
- *could be because he's 'different'*
- *possibly quarrelled with others*
- *hiding a secret*
- *rejected by his family because lies have been told about him.*

Discussion:
- *on the one hand – caused his own problems by his actions/personality*
- *on the other hand – badly treated by society, both by village and family*
- *writer has succeeded in convincing the reader one way or another*
- *on balance: more to blame or less to blame?*

This sketch of an answer provides a relevant argument. It will, incidentally, have covered the other essential skills below.

3 Select evidence to support your argument

You will have provided evidence of setting, events, etc. to back up each of the points made in the sketch of the answer above. You haven't included anything irrelevant to the question.

4 Analyse the effect of language/filmic techniques

You will have done this because you have been dealing with characterisation and central concerns throughout, and possibly with setting and dialogue.

5 Engage with the text and the question

You will have faced the question head on and used your knowledge of the text to demonstrate how you have reached your conclusion.

6 Evaluate the effectiveness of the text with respect to the question

In your discussion of the extent to which the writer convinces you, for example, to be sympathetic or unsympathetic with the main character, you will have shown that you have made an evaluation of the text.

7 Write in a technically accurate way

After all that, you just have to check the accuracy of your writing – this is important because if it doesn't measure up to the definition of technical accuracy (page 134), you will fail.

Example 2

If we look at another question using the same imaginary text as on page 135, the argument will be of a totally different shape.

(?) Question

- Choose a novel with an incident involving two main characters that creates a turning point in the novel. Describe the incident and show to what extent the outcome for each character makes a satisfactory ending to the novel.

> ## Hints & tips ⭐
>
> *To answer any of the questions in Section 2, you may use:*
> - *a specified Scottish text in Section 2, as long as it is a different genre from the question you answered in Section 1*
> - *any other Scottish text you have been taught in a different genre*
> - *any text in English (including in translation) and from any period in a different genre*
> - *film or television drama from anywhere in the world.*

The argument could look something like this:

Character X confronts character Y and informs him that he (X) is going to tell the whole story of the scam and his sister to his family.

So, Y:
- *uses X's eccentric personality and his supposed past misdemeanours to discredit him*
- *convinces the family to reject X*
- *gains something he wants – money/woman?*

but
- *perhaps not what he thought it would be (guilt taints his future success)*
- *character X tries to reinstate himself with his family*

but
- *because of Y's lies is rejected*

therefore
- *X slips back into isolation even more damaged than before.*

Conclusion: the writer has shown that each of the characters has flaws and, although Y may think he has won, both deserve some part in their fates.

This sketch of an answer provides a relevant argument and again you have dealt with the other essential skills below.

3 Select evidence to support your argument

The selection of evidence is different. Very little material from before the incident is used. Character Y's part has to be dealt with, as well as character X's part and the family situation gains much more prominence.

You will have provided evidence to back up each of the points made in the sketch of the answer above, but you won't have included anything irrelevant to the question.

4 Analyse the effect of language/filmic techniques

You will have done this because you have been dealing with characterisation and central concerns throughout, and also conflict/contrast.

5 Engage with the text and the question

You will have faced the question head on and used your knowledge of the text to demonstrate how you have reached your conclusion.

6 Evaluate the effectiveness of the text with respect to the question

In your discussion of the extent to which the writer convinces you that they deserve their fates, you will have shown that you have made an evaluation of the text.

These **two** examples of **very different essays** on the same imaginary text should illustrate three important pieces of advice about answering questions:

1 There is **no point in swotting up a possible critical essay in advance** of seeing the questions.

2 **Analysis is not an add-on or a list of techniques** that have to be covered: relevant analysis occurs throughout your essay, when you are discussing the effectiveness of characterisation or a central concern in the course of your answer.

3 **There is no formula** that works for all texts and all questions.

Hints & tips

It is bad practice to start your answer by picking two or three features from the box at the head of the section and then using these features as building blocks for your answer. For example, if you pick out characterisation and theme, and then try to answer by dealing with 'character' in isolation and follow that by doing the same with 'theme', you will end up repeating yourself and the chances are that the answer to the question you have actually been asked will have disappeared down the cracks. It is an especially unwise approach in poetry questions because it leads to a fragmented repetitive approach to a poem, looking at 'techniques' individually for their own sake instead of using them at relevant points in the development of your answer to the question.

Acquiring good knowledge of your texts

This involves three stages: **collecting**, **organising** and **learning**.

In the previous pages we have looked at the basic skills needed to answer a question, but you can't begin to select the relevant material if you don't know your text really well and, more importantly, can remember it.

Stage 1 Collecting your materials

Your materials will include the following:

a) **The primary source** is the text itself. There is no substitute for reading the text, but the reading must be active, not passive. Active reading involves reading the text again for the specific purpose of making notes on the main characters, or for looking for useful quotations. Passive reading would simply involve reading the text through without any purpose to keep your brain alert. It is useful to have a pencil in your hand as you are reading a text, either to make notes or to mark (lightly if it's a school book!) important pages to return to.

b) **Your notes on the text** – notes you have taken or been given in class and notes you have made later. The notes you have made for yourself will be more useful than other people's notes because you will have had to understand what you are writing down, whereas you might not exactly understand the notes your friend has taken.

c) **Your memory of what other people have said about the text**, what you feel about the text, any discussions you have had on the text.

Hints & tips

There is no point in trying to second guess what the question for your text might be — there is too large a variety of possible questions. There is even less point in writing an all-purpose essay on your text, preparing it and then using it regardless of the question. Even when you try to 'wrap' the essay round with little references to the question in the hope that the marker might think that you are answering the question, it doesn't work. A first paragraph, which looks as if it is going to answer the question and then little add-ons at the end of each paragraph are not at all convincing, and cannot turn an irrelevant answer into a relevant one. By all means practise writing critical essays, but don't assume that you can use any of them again in the exam.

Useful ideas come up in discussion, but if you don't write them down at the time, you may forget what was said.

d) **Commercially produced notes** – but make sure that you understand what the writer is saying. Don't quote an opinion if you don't know what it means. You are likely to betray your ignorance.

e) **Notes you have found in your research on the internet** – but remember to check the credentials of the site you happen to be looking at. There will be simple stuff that you can understand, which might be wrong, or there may be complicated criticism that you don't understand fully.

f) **Essays you have written about the text** – but these are less useful than you would think, because they are not answers to the question you will be asked in the exam.

Stage 2 Organising your materials

Basic organisation means having all these notes available in a large file, but there are ways of sorting the material and your thoughts at the same time.

a) **Lists and tables**

One of the simplest methods is simply to gather your ideas into lists under basic headings:

- **Who?** – characters
- **What?** – the events/incidents of the play/story/poem/film
- **How?** – the techniques: structure/narrative point of view/language, etc.
- **Why?** – the questions we ask of the text: what is it really 'about' – its central concerns
- **Where?** – setting in place
- **When?** – setting in time.

A suggested version of this method is illustrated on page 143. It can be adapted for all genres except non-fiction. An example for non-fiction is given on page 140.

b) **Diagrams**

Another simple method is to use a **spider diagram**. This suits people who are more spatial in their thinking and less likely to remember lists. The key is only to add to the diagram when you gain more knowledge of your text as you go through the year.

An example diagram is illustrated on page 141. This example can be adapted to suit novels, short stories, drama, film and TV studies. A second version more suited to poetry is shown at the top of page 142.

An example for non-fiction is given at the foot of page 142.

The following diagrams have been developed to a detailed stage – but there is no reason why you wouldn't stop at the first level, just to get the main points clear in your head. There are many other methods and templates you can use – the important thing is that you try to get your thoughts in some kind of order by writing them down in a pattern you can understand.

Table for all genres except non-fiction

WHO?	WHAT?	HOW?	WHY?	WHERE/WHEN?
MAIN CHARACTERS	**PLOT**	**STRUCTURE**	**QUESTION THE TEXT**	**SETTING**
1 Name	**1 Opening: introduction of characters**	Chapters/scenes/sequences/acts/incidents/flashbacks (if important)	What is the text 'about': its central concerns?	Place
a) Relationships/conflicts			• social	
b) Main characteristics			• political	Society
c) Character development	**2 Turning points**	**CLIMAX/END/DÉNOUEMENT** (effectiveness)	• historical	
2 Name			• moral	Time
a)	**3 Key incidents**	**NARRATIVE** (1st/3rd/dual/framed/narrator/(un)reliable, (if important))	• emotional	
b)			• psychological	Period
c)	**4 Ending/dénouement**		• etc.	
3) Name, etc.				
IMPORTANT QUOTATIONS	**IMPORTANT QUOTATIONS**	**TECHNIQUES/FEATURES/NOVEL/SHORT STORY**	**IMPORTANT QUOTATIONS**	**IMPORTANT FOR CHARACTER?**
		• language		**IMPORTANT FOR CENTRAL CONCERNS?**
	DRAMA ← PLUS	• tone		
	• dialogue	• register	_PLUS → FILM/TV DRAMA_	
	• soliloquy	• symbolism	• _mise en scène_	
	• aspects of staging	• mood	• editing	
	• etc.	• atmosphere.	• use of camera	
MINOR CHARACTERS			• etc.	**POSSIBLE QUOTATIONS**
Names/relationships				

Diagram for fiction/drama/film

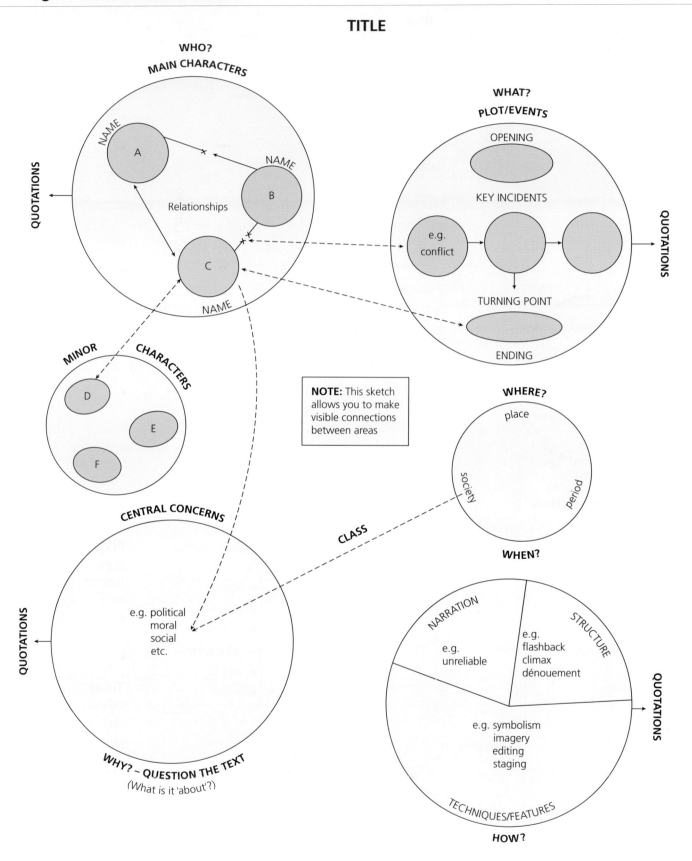

TITLE

WHO?
MAIN CHARACTERS

NAME

A

NAME

B

Relationships

C

NAME

QUOTATIONS

WHAT?
PLOT/EVENTS

OPENING

KEY INCIDENTS

e.g.
conflict

TURNING POINT

ENDING

QUOTATIONS

MINOR CHARACTERS

D

E

F

NOTE: This sketch allows you to make visible connections between areas

WHERE?
place

society

period

WHEN?

CENTRAL CONCERNS

e.g. political
moral
social
etc.

QUOTATIONS

CLASS

WHY? – QUESTION THE TEXT
(What is it 'about'?)

NARRATION
e.g.
unreliable

STRUCTURE
e.g.
flashback
climax
dénouement

e.g. symbolism
imagery
editing
staging

QUOTATIONS

TECHNIQUES/FEATURES

HOW?

Diagram for poetry

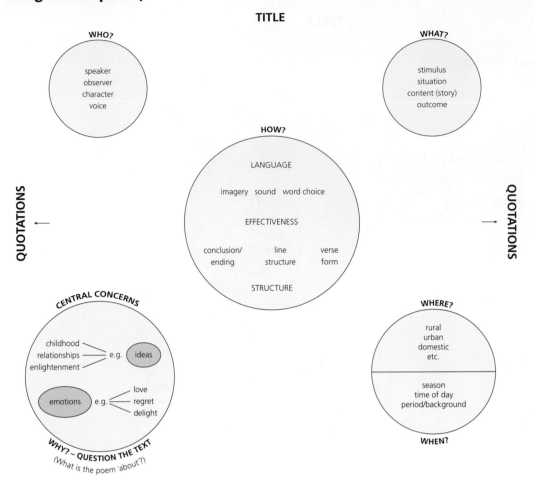

Table for non-fiction

WHO?	WHAT?	HOW?	WHY?	WHERE/WHEN?
Names	Topic	Narrative voice	Purpose/central concerns:	**Place:** geographic familiar exotic etc.
		Writer's stance	● social	
			● political	
Characteristics	Events	Sources	● historical	
			● educational	
			● moral	
		Evidence	● etc.	**Time:** period of history type of society etc.
	Conclusion			
		Technique/features:		
		● language		
		● tone		
		● rhetoric		
QUOTATIONS	**QUOTATIONS**	**QUOTATIONS**	**QUOTATIONS**	**QUOTATIONS**

There are three advantages of structuring notes in any of these forms:

- You have to think hard about your text to fill them in.
- The act of filling them in fixes them in your mind.
- They can be quickly surveyed when you come to revise.

Stage 3 Learning your materials

If you look around you will find, or you may have been taught, various kinds of study skills to help you with your learning/revision. The important thing is that you are learning the right material, and for the Critical Essay you have to know:

a) the content of your text

b) the possible ways in which you can classify your knowledge for easy selection

c) some quotations for use as evidence of your detailed knowledge of the text.

These three things should be in a readily accessible form so that you can quickly survey it all and remind yourself of the main ideas. This material should not be buried in a big file of loose papers, but organised on cards, diagrams, coloured highlighted sheets, a file on your PC (backed up!) or papered to your bedroom wall. Whatever is easiest for you.

There is some memory work involved, but the real work is done in the thinking time you put in to create your notes. Other people's notes won't do. The words have to pass through **your** brain on the way from the text to the paper to be of any use to you.

Hints & tips ★

Very recent research suggests that you think differently when you write, as opposed to type, and that you retain the information for longer.

Summary

1 Organising your material means you are actively engaged in learning. You are not just passively reading through your text – again!
2 Have your notes in an easily accessible form for quick scanning and revising.

Advice about quotations

Memorable quotations are likely to be quite short. It is better to have a number of short quotations that you have a chance of remembering than two or three long quotations.

Try to make your quotations do more than one task. A quotation revealing character could also be useful in talking about a central concern. And a quotation dealing with a crucial point in the text will probably be about plot, character and central concerns.

When you choose your important quotations for your notes, you are actually working to deepen your understanding of the text. It is probable that you will not use all the quotations you have chosen, because the question you answer will usually require some selection of your material (including your quotations), but the effort will not have been wasted.

You should perhaps aim for about seven or eight really useful quotations per text. Poetry maybe requires a little more detail.

A very short quotation is easily incorporated into a sentence as evidence (see the example from *Macbeth* on page 155). All you need to do is put quotation marks round the actual words quoted. If the quotation you want to use is longer than that – maybe two lines of poetry – then you should start a new line for the beginning of the quotation, use quotation marks and start a new line after the quotation (see the example from 'Church Going' on page 153). Watch your punctuation after a quotation. Often, you want to say 'This shows … ', which is the beginning of a new sentence so 'This' needs to start with a capital letter.

Remember that you can refer to actions and incidents in the text as well as, or instead of, quoting directly – especially in longer texts.

Now that you know the material, we can start applying your hard-won knowledge to the exam paper in front of you. The next section looks at how best to use your knowledge with respect to:
- **reading the questions**
- **choosing the questions**
- **answering the questions.**

Reading the questions

There are two parts to each of the questions. The important part – the **real question** – is the **second part**. The first part is just an introduction defining the texts that will be suitable for the question.

Example 1

Choose a novel or short story in which there is a key incident of high tension between two of the characters.

With reference to appropriate techniques, describe the incident and discuss how the outcome of the incident affects the fate of the characters in the course of the novel or short story.

The first part gets you to think if your novel has such an incident in it. As most novels involve conflict of some sort, it is highly probable that your novel will 'fit'.

But the **second part** is the **real question**. It tells you what you have **actually to do**, in this case:
- 'Describe the incident' suggests that you have to know this part of the novel extremely well so that you can refer to it.
- 'Discuss how' requires you to be able to trace the fates of the characters as they have been affected by that particular incident.

Perhaps the real question – the second part – is harder than you thought when you looked simply at the introduction to the question.

Example 2

Choose a play in which a distortion of the truth (such as lies, disguise or mistaken identity) causes problems for one of the main characters.

With reference to appropriate techniques, briefly explain what the distortion of the truth is and then discuss how the dramatist's presentation of the character's problems enhances your understanding of character in the play as a whole.

In the second part:

- 'Briefly explain' is just asking you to define the nature of the distortion and what problems it causes.
- 'dramatist's presentation' – this is really asking you about characterisation and how the character copes with the problem – successfully or unsuccessfully, for example.
- 'enhances your understanding of character in the play as a whole' means you have to put this 'character/problem' idea into the context of the play as a whole. What effect, for example, does it have on the outcome? What does the exploration of the idea have to tell you about a central concern of the play?

Example 3

Choose a novel or short story in which a specific feature such as setting, structure, narrative voice or symbolism is an important feature of the novel or short story.

With reference to appropriate techniques, discuss how the writer uses this feature in the novel or short story and how it enhances your appreciation of the text as a whole.

In the first part the list of features is an 'open' list – 'feature such as' suggests that you can use any of the features of fiction you choose in order to answer this question.

In the second part:

- 'Discuss how the writer uses this feature' is fairly straightforward.
- '[Discuss] how this feature…enhances your appreciation of the text as a whole' means that you need to show how the use of, for example, symbolism deepens your response to the text by possibly creating something of wider significance to underline one of the central concerns. For example, the conch in *Lord of the Flies* becomes inextricably fused with the whole central concern of democracy versus dictatorship.

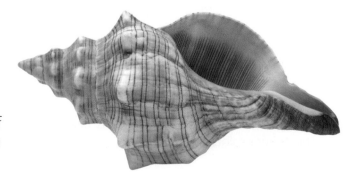

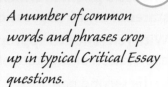

Hints & tips

A number of common words and phrases crop up in typical Critical Essay questions.

- ✓ *describe the incident*
- ✓ *briefly explain*
- ✓ *dramatist's/ novelist's/poet's/ writer's presentation*
- ✓ *enhances your understanding of X in the play as a whole*
- ✓ *enhances your appreciation of the text as a whole*
- ✓ *discuss how the writer uses this feature*
- ✓ *discuss how the poet's exploration of*
- ✓ *deepened your understanding*
- ✓ *by referring in detail*
- ✓ *how the writer creates*
- ✓ *how the writer conveys*
- ✓ *adds to your understanding of the central concerns/ appreciation of the text as a whole*
- ✓ *makes you aware of (by use of characterisation, incident, gradual revelation, etc.).*

Make sure that you are familiar with what each instruction asks you to do.

Example 4

Choose a poem in which the poet explores one of the following states of mind: depression, indecision, optimism, celebration.

With reference to appropriate techniques, discuss how the poet's exploration of the state of mind has deepened your understanding of it.

In the second part:

- 'Discuss how the poet's exploration of' means you must look at the ways in which the poet opens up the idea of the state of mind.
- 'deepened your understanding' means you need to discuss how the poem created new insight for you about the state of mind.

Choosing the questions

You have to choose **one** question in **Section 2** and it must be from a **different** genre from the one you answered in Section 1 – Scottish text.

Drama, fiction and poetry

Below is a sample of Section 2 questions on drama, fiction and poetry to illustrate the task of choosing the best question for your text(s). Questions 7, 8 and 9 (non-fiction) and 13, 14 and 15 (film and television drama) are given on pages 157–158.

Questions

Drama

1   Choose a play in which one scene brings about a reversal of fortune for one of the characters.

   With reference to appropriate techniques, discuss how this reversal of fortune makes the character's fate inevitable.

2   Choose a play that has as one of its main concerns loss – such as loss of respect, honour or status.

   With reference to appropriate techniques, briefly explain what the loss is and discuss how the dramatist's exploration of this loss is important to your appreciation of the play as a whole.

3   Choose a play that deals with a conflict such as that between families, generations, couples or social classes.

   With reference to appropriate techniques, describe the conflict and discuss how the outcome of the conflict affects your appreciation of the play as a whole.

Prose: fiction

4   Choose a novel or short story in which there is a conflict based on power, love or wealth.

   With reference to appropriate techniques, explain how the conflict affects the characters and discuss how the writer explores the idea of power, love or wealth in the text as a whole. ⇨

5 Choose a novel or short story that has a powerful ending.

With reference to appropriate techniques, discuss how the ending acts as a satisfactory outcome to the novel or short story.

6 Choose a novel or short story in which a central character displays strength of mind in dealing with the difficulties which face her or him.

With reference to appropriate techniques, discuss how the writer makes you aware of the character's strengths, and how these strengths influence the outcome for the character.

Prose: non-fiction

Questions 7, 8 and 9 are on page 157.

Poetry

10 Choose a poem in which the speaker experiences a moment of revelation or understanding.

With reference to appropriate techniques, describe what the moment was about and discuss how the experience or revelation is important to the poem as a whole.

11 Choose a poem in which the poet creates a convincing character.

With reference to appropriate techniques, explain how the poet's technical skill brings the character alive in a convincing way.

12 Choose a poem which deals with the serious aspect of life or a serious subject.

With reference to appropriate techniques, discuss how the poet's presentation of this has increased your understanding of the aspect or subject.

Film and television drama

Questions 13, 14 and 15 are on pages 157–158.

Let's assume that you have answered Section 1 – Scottish text by doing a text from the Poetry genre.

Remember

You might have answered on 'Originally' by Carol Ann Duffy. That means that you can't use:

☞ 'Originally'
☞ another poem by Carol Ann Duffy
☞ another poem from the specified selection of Scottish texts
☞ a poem at all — Scottish or from anywhere else in the world.

As well as the poetry you have just answered on in Section 1, let's assume you have studied both a novel and a play, so you now have to look at the first six questions in Section 2 to see which one of these six questions is best for you.

(?) Question 1

Choose a play in which one scene brings about a reversal of fortune for one of the characters.

If you look only at the first part of the question, you can probably think of a scene in the play you have studied which fits that definition. But, as described above, you must look at what you are being asked to **do** in the second part.

With reference to appropriate techniques, discuss how this reversal of fortune makes the character's fate inevitable.

You have to have in mind **one** important scene which is **crucial** to the fate of the character. Perhaps the play you have in mind does not have such a distinct and isolated scene of reversal. If so, this question might not be the best choice for your play.

(?) Question 2

Choose a play that has as one of its main concerns loss – such as loss of respect, honour or status.

This question might be better. If your character has suffered a 'reversal of fortune', it is likely that this will have involved a loss of some kind, so your play will 'fit'.

Now look at the **real** question, the one you actually have to answer:

With reference to appropriate techniques, briefly explain what the loss is and discuss how the dramatist's exploration of this loss is important to your appreciation of the play as a whole.

You don't have the problem in this question of having to know a particular scene in detail so, on the whole, it is probably an easier choice than question 1.

You would now look at question 3 to see what it offers – remembering to look carefully at the second part of the question.

(?) Question 3

Choose a play that deals with a conflict such as that between families, generations, couples or social classes.

With reference to appropriate techniques, describe the conflict and discuss how the outcome of the conflict affects your appreciation of the play as a whole.

- 'Describe' is fairly straightforward and gives you an easy entry to your essay.
- 'How the outcome of the conflict affects your appreciation' – this may concern whether you feel that the outcome is satisfactory, in the sense that the way in which the play develops leads to a 'right' ending, even though it may be a tragic ending for the characters.

(?) Question 4

Choose a novel or short story in which there is a conflict based on power, love or wealth.

With reference to appropriate techniques, explain how the conflict affects the characters and discuss how the writer explores the idea of power, love or wealth in the text as a whole.

The key point to consider here is if a conflict of this kind exists. If it does, you then have to be able to 'explain how …' and 'discuss how the writer explores …' in the light of 'the text as a whole'.

(?) Question 5

Choose a novel or short story that has a powerful ending.

With reference to appropriate techniques, discuss how the ending acts as a satisfactory outcome to the novel or short story.

The key point here is whether the ending is powerful enough. If it is, then you have to be able to discuss in what way the ending is satisfactory. But remember that 'satisfactory' does not necessarily mean 'happy' – see notes on question 3 on page 148.

(?) Question 6

Choose a novel or short story in which a central character displays strength of mind in dealing with the difficulties which face her or him.

With reference to appropriate techniques, discuss how the writer makes you aware of the character's strengths, and how these strengths influence the outcome for the character.

The key point to consider here is whether you have a central character who has strength of mind. If you have a character who fits this description you then have to consider the phrases in the second half of the question:

- 'makes you aware of …'
- 'how these strengths influence the outcome …'.

Answering the questions

The **six points** below will help you to answer the questions.

1 **Opening paragraph** – this should signal what the main thrust of your line of thought is going to be. It should not:
 - simply repeat the question
 - make statements such as 'I am going to discuss …'
 - list techniques or features (unless specifically asked for in the question). This practice may weaken your essay because it dictates a mechanical structure that does not allow you the flexibility to create an argument. It can cause you to lose sight of the central concerns. The discussion of techniques should take place naturally in the course of developing a line of thought in the answer.

Hints & tips ⭐

Remember that the first part of the question is just an introduction defining the texts that will be suitable for the question.

*In the second part, and **only** in the second part of the question, if you think it helps, you could underline or use a highlighter to mark the important instructions. If you do it **only** for the second part of the question then you will be able to see the real task ahead of you, which will help you to come to a conclusion about your choice of question.*

If you have only one other text left after Section 1, you only have to look at the three relevant questions in that text's genre.

2 **Concluding paragraph** – this should reach the logical end-point of your argument, e.g. 'Hamlet has finally succeeded in avenging his father's death, although at a heavy price'. It should not:
- simply restate the question
- make statements such as 'I have shown how …'. If your line of thought is sound, you will have shown this. And if your line of thought is not sound, a statement such as this will not make it so.

3 **Reordering/selecting your material** – most questions demand a degree of this.
- Some questions will have a focus, which means that some of the material you have at your disposal will be not be needed.
- Some questions demand that you start from the middle of the text, or even from the end.

4 **Central concern(s)** – all questions require you to show your understanding of the central concern(s) of the text, even where this is not spelt out in the question.

5 **Quotation/reference**
- In shorter texts, such as poems, you are more likely to be able to quote and comment readily from important parts of the poem or short story which are relevant to your answer.
- In longer texts, you might be more likely to make reference to the text by means of describing specific events or incidents. Close analysis of particular words and phrases is rarely necessary. There may be times in a more 'technical' question on a novel or in poetry or film where detailed (and meaningful) analytical comment is appropriate. The question itself will make it clear if this is needed.

6 **Technical features** – there is a box at the top of each genre that reminds you of a number of features of the genre. The list is an open list – it says 'such as' – so any other features that you wish to comment on are entirely acceptable, if they are relevant to the question you have been asked. It is not intended to be a list of items that you 'should' put into your essay. See point 1 above and also *Hints & tips* on page 138.

Remember

Don't forget to check your technical accuracy (see page 134).

The following pages give three demonstrations of these six points, using question 10 (poetry), question 3 (drama) and question 5 (prose: fiction) from the sample question bank on pages 146–147.

Example 1 Poetry

Church Going by Philip Larkin

You may not have come across this poem, 'Church Going', before in class, but if you read it now you should find that you can see how the question should be tackled – and you will have the pleasure of reading a good poem.

Church Going

Once I am sure there's nothing going on

I step inside, letting the door thud shut.

Another church: matting, seats, and stone,

And little books; sprawlings of flowers, cut

5   For Sunday, brownish now; some brass and stuff

Up at the holy end; the small neat organ;

And a tense, musty, unignorable silence,

Brewed God knows how long. Hatless, I take off

My cycle-clips in awkward reverence.

10 Move forward, run my hand around the font.

From where I stand, the roof looks almost new –

Cleaned, or restored? Someone would know: I don't.

Mounting the lectern, I peruse a few

Hectoring large-scale verses, and pronounce

15 'Here endeth' much more loudly than I'd meant.

The echoes snigger briefly. Back at the door

I sign the book, donate an Irish sixpence,

Reflect the place was not worth stopping for.

Yet stop I did: in fact I often do,

20 And always end much at a loss like this,

Wondering what to look for; wondering, too,

When churches will fall completely out of use

What we shall turn them into, if we shall keep

A few cathedrals chronically on show,

25 Their parchment, plate and pyx in locked cases,

And let the rest rent-free to rain and sheep.

Shall we avoid them as unlucky places?

Or, after dark, will dubious women come

To make their children touch a particular stone;

30 Pick simples for a cancer; or on some

Advised night see walking a dead one?

Power of some sort will go on

In games, in riddles, seemingly at random;

But superstition, like belief, must die,

35 And what remains when disbelief has gone?

Grass, weedy pavement, brambles, buttress, sky,

A shape less recognisable each week,

A purpose more obscure. I wonder who

Will be the last, the very last, to seek

40 This place for what it was; one of the crew

That tap and jot and know what rood-lofts were?

Some ruin-bibber, randy for antique,

Or Christmas-addict, counting on a whiff

Of gown-and-bands and organ-pipes and myrrh?

45 Or will he be my representative,

Bored, uninformed, knowing the ghostly silt

Dispersed, yet tending to this cross of ground

Through suburb scrub because it held unspilt

So long and equably what since is found

50 Only in separation – marriage, and birth,

And death, and thoughts of these – for which was built

This special shell? For, though I've no idea

What this accoutred frowsty barn is worth,

It pleases me to stand in silence here;

55 A serious house on serious earth it is,

In whose blent air all our compulsions meet,

Are recognised, and robed as destinies.

And that much never can be obsolete,

Since someone will forever be surprising

60 A hunger in himself to be more serious,

And gravitating with it to this ground,

Which, he once heard, was proper to grow wise in,

If only that so many dead lie round.

Philip Larkin

? Question

Choose a poem in which the speaker experiences a moment of revelation or understanding.

With reference to appropriate techniques, describe what the moment was about and discuss how the experience or revelation is important to the poem as a whole.

Answer

Below is an outline answer using the six points for 'Answering the questions' on pages 149–150.

1 **Opening paragraph**
   In the poem 'Church Going' by Philip Larkin there is a moment towards the end of the poem when the speaker says:
   'It pleases me to stand in silence here;
   A serious house on serious earth it is,'
   He finally comes to a sort of conclusion that religion might just have something to say even to a modern agnostic/atheist such as he is. It is important because in the whole poem up to that point he has been questioning the point of churches and religion in the modern world.

2 **Concluding paragraph**
   The importance of the moment is that it causes us to question our own views on religion. With Larkin we have looked at the parts of the church and its rituals that seem to have no use, but his speaker's revelation suggests that there is in people a hunger for spiritual things and that the church might provide at least a place for deep thought.

3 **Reordering/selecting your material**
   In this question an answer really has to start near the end of the poem and then go back to consider the earlier part of the poem.

4 **Central concern(s)**
   The central concern is almost dictated by the question – some sort of hunger for spirituality would be acceptable as a central concern. But there are other possibilities: that such attempts at seeking answers ultimately fail – if you think the last line undercuts everything he has seemed to say. There are many ways of reading any poem and no single, absolutely cast-iron, interpretation.

5 **Quotation/reference**
   The opening paragraph contains a two-line quotation, and in the body of the answer there will be the need to quote, for example, 'some brass and stuff' when discussing the uselessness of some church rituals – 'stuff' being a particularly good example of word choice in this context as it suggests in itself a pile of useless things that nobody can be bothered looking at closely.

153

6 Technical features

The opening and closing paragraphs illustrated above deal with 'central concerns', and a feature such as word choice has been illustrated in point 5. Features such as these should appear in the course of the essay where they are needed to expand on a point you are making in the course of your argument. But not every quotation needs to be analysed to

death. You may wish to quote in support of a 'psychological' point. For example:
'Yet stop I did: in fact I often do,
And always end much at a loss like this,'
shows how the rather cynical speaker of the first two stanzas is perhaps not quite so sure of his views as he thought. This quotation makes a 'character' point and does not need further analysis.

Remember

Don't forget to check your technical accuracy (see page 134).

Example 2 Drama

Macbeth by William Shakespeare

Drama is harder to demonstrate than other genres because if you haven't studied the play chosen for this purpose, it will be less helpful. But it is easy to find a synopsis of a play, and that might help to make the next example more useful.

Macbeth is one of the better known of Shakespeare's tragedies. If you look at a synopsis at www.shakespeare-online.com/plays or the Wikipedia article on *Macbeth* (Plot), you should be able to follow the main points of this answer.

? Question

Choose a play that deals with a conflict such as that between families, generations, couples or social classes.

With reference to appropriate techniques, describe the conflict and discuss how the outcome of the conflict affects your appreciation of the play as a whole.

Answer

1 Opening paragraph
In *Macbeth* by William Shakespeare there is a conflict between Macbeth and his wife which ends only with their deaths but, in a sense, their deaths allow Shakespeare in the ending of the play to suggest a better and more settled future for Scotland.

2 Concluding paragraph
At the end of the play Macbeth manages to salvage some of his honourable qualities by refusing to surrender to Malcolm, and dying 'with harness on our back' (i.e. in armour, as a soldier). Although the couple have been in conflict throughout the play, Macbeth still

feels great grief when he hears of her death, and it adds to his sense of his inevitable fate, which is sealed in the final scene.

3 **Reordering/selecting your material**

In this case, the order of the material will follow roughly the chronological events of the play, but the selection will be much more important. If you know the play or have read the synopsis, the conflict between Macbeth and Lady Macbeth is followed in only a few, very important, scenes – the letter from Macbeth/the decision or persuasion to Duncan's murder/the murder and its aftermath. The next conflict is over Macbeth's plan to murder Banquo and Fleance – Macbeth does not take her fully into his confidence. The next important scene is the banquet scene, where Lady Macbeth watches Macbeth almost come to pieces and creates a diversion. After that, there is only the reported sleepwalking/the sleepwalking scene and then the news of Lady Macbeth's death just as Macbeth is about to take part in his last battle. Selection is really important. There are large areas of the play that could lead you into irrelevance.

4 **Central concern(s)**

You will have been talking of concerns such as conflict, honour, ambition, cruelty, etc. as you write your answer.

5 **Quotation/reference**

Some really important parts could be illustrated by direct quotation: 'Screw your courage to the sticking-place,/And we'll not fail'; 'To know my deed, 'twere best not know myself'; 'Be innocent of the knowledge, dearest chuck'; something from the banquet scene; 'The thane of Fife, had a wife: where is she now?'; 'She should have died hereafter;/there would have been a time for such a word'; something from Macbeth's speech after her death – 'Tomorrow, and tomorrow, and tomorrow …' and something from the end – see concluding paragraph. You only need six or seven short quotations. Other references will be to events and incidents chosen to show how the conflict in the relationship plays out.

6 **Technical features**

In your answer you will have been dealing with characterisation, conflict, central concerns, possibly dialogue and perhaps climax, all quite naturally. You don't need to drag in other features just to 'analyse'. You have been engaged in analysis and evaluation throughout your answer.

Remember

Don't forget to check your technical accuracy (see page 134).

Author's note: if you want to see what might have happened if Lady Macbeth had remained alive, read David Greig's excellent play *Dunsinane*.

Example 3 Prose fiction

The Great Gatsby by F. Scott Fitzgerald

For a novel, the method is similar. This time the example is *The Great Gatsby* by F. Scott Fitzgerald. A brief synopsis can be found on Wikipedia or a longer, more detailed and fairly accurate one on www.cliffnotes.com.

? Question

Choose a novel or short story that has a powerful ending.

With reference to appropriate techniques, discuss how the ending acts as a satisfactory outcome to the novel or short story.

Answer

1 **Opening paragraph**
   The Great Gatsby ends with Gatsby's death at the hands of George Wilson, who blames him for the death of his wife, Myrtle. Gatsby is innocent but takes the blame for Daisy, who he has loved and just lost. The fact that he has failed to realise his great dream, which has been to regain Daisy's love by becoming as rich as her husband, Tom, and to take her away from him, leaves Gatsby in limbo, his dream destroyed, his whole future a blank. Thus his sacrifice for her finally gives his death some point.

2 **Concluding paragraph**
   This paragraph would deal with your final evaluative comment about the extent to which Gatsby's end was 'satisfactory'; you might include a reference to the fact that almost no one attended his funeral as evidence for your opinion either way.

3 **Reordering/selecting your material**
   Here, you have to start with the ending and then decide how far back you want to go to deal with the whole novel. You would probably select material about how he loved and lost Daisy, how

the narrator, Nick, lets you see Gatsby through his eyes, and how Nick regarded Gatsby in the end: 'You're worth the whole damn bunch put together.'

4 **Central concern(s)**
   One or two of the central concerns – the power of wealth, unattainable dreams, exploitation of little people like Myrtle and George, the carelessness of the rich, etc. – are likely to have been touched on.

5 **Quotation/reference**
   Again, as with a play, you could have a small number of key quotations at your fingertips, but mainly you have to refer in detail to important incidents/conversations/settings.

6 **Technical features**
   In your answer you will have been dealing with characterisation, the effect of the narrator, central concerns, possibly dialogue and perhaps climax, all quite naturally. You don't need to drag in other features just to 'analyse'. You have been engaged in analysis and evaluation throughout your answer.

Remember

Don't forget to check for technical accuracy (see page 134).

Summary

1 Make sure you read the question carefully before you choose to do it.
2 Get straight to grips with the question in the first paragraph.
3 Select and order your material. You won't be able to use all you know.
4 Your conclusion should arise from the argument of your answer, and will probably contain an overall evaluation of the text and question.
5 Check your technical accuracy.

Non-fiction and film and television drama

Remember the restriction about genres. You cannot answer on non-fiction if you have answered on a Scottish prose text (novel or short story) in Section 1. However, you are perfectly free to choose film and television drama because it does not appear in Section 1.

Questions

Prose: non-fiction

7 Choose a piece of journalism that is concerned with an important contemporary issue – economic, social or political.

With reference to appropriate techniques, discuss how the writer, by her or his presentation of ideas and evidence, increases your knowledge and understanding of the issue.

8 Choose a book, journal or account which conveys a sense of an exciting, harrowing or dangerous experience.

With reference to appropriate techniques, discuss how the writer's use of features such as setting, climax and language were important elements in your appreciation of the experience.

9 Choose a work of biography or autobiography that discusses a problem or problems which the subject has had to face.

With reference to appropriate techniques, briefly describe the problem(s) and discuss how the writer's presentation of the problem(s) creates sympathy for the subject.

Film and television drama

13 Choose a film or television drama that has at its centre a destructive personality.

With reference to appropriate techniques, discuss how the destructive nature of the character is revealed and how this affects your view of the character in the course of the film or television drama. ⇨

Hints & tips

Non-fiction

The features of a non-fiction text are more like the features that were discussed in the chapters dealing with the Understanding, Analysis and Evaluation paper.

✓ The writer's stance is particularly important. You should be able to detect from the tone and language which 'view' he/she is promoting.
✓ The evidence – is it convincing?
✓ Is the evidence selective – does it seem to be one-sided?
✓ Is the language emotive – are you persuaded to admire or to condemn?

14   Choose a film or television drama in which a key scene or sequence is intensified by sound and/or visual effects.

With reference to appropriate techniques, describe how the sound/visual effects intensify the scene or sequence and discuss the importance of the scene to the film or television drama as a whole.

15   Choose a film or television drama that explores a particular stage of life such as childhood or adolescence.

With reference to appropriate techniques, discuss how the film or programme-makers explore the subject and how they create a convincing depiction of that stage of life.

The last two examples use question 8 (prose: non fiction) and question 13 (film and television drama) from the sample question bank above to demonstrate the six points on pages 149–150.

Example 4 Prose: non-fiction

Touching the Void by Joe Simpson

This book by a mountaineer and philosopher deals with his account of a disastrous expedition to the Peruvian Andes. Wikipedia has a summary and you can find a slightly longer one at sites such as www.bookrags.com.

(?) Question

Choose a book, journal or account which conveys a sense of an exciting, harrowing or dangerous experience.

With reference to appropriate techniques, discuss how the writer's use of features such as setting, climax and language were important elements in your appreciation of the experience.

Answer

1   **Opening paragraph**

In *Touching the Void* by Joe Simpson, the writer's ability to recreate his experience is illustrated in his description of the setting on the mountain, his creating of climax – both the moral climax of the book and the physical climax which continues the suspense – and his precise use of word choice and imagery.

2   **Concluding paragraph**

The economical structure of the book – the fact that it starts when they are already on the mountain and finishes with a swift summary of the aftermath of the incident – allows the real focus to fall on the moral dilemma at the heart of the book. What is left seared on the reader's mind is the emotional and realistic description of the painful return, with the associated suspense as to its outcome.

3   **Reordering/selecting your material**

In this case, a chronological approach would allow discussion of some of the suggested techniques and any other possible techniques you might think of (for example, the technical and detailed mountaineering vocabulary lends verisimilitude).

4   **Central concern(s)**

The central concerns – moral responsibility, supremacy of willpower – will have been part of your argument.

5   **Quotation/reference**

If you choose to deal with description of the setting, word choice or imagery, you would need to have some quotations to illustrate your points.

6   **Technical features**

In the course of your answer you will have dealt with structure, climax, setting and possibly language. The question in this case actually demands that you cover a number of features, which you have achieved.

Example 5 Film and television drama

The Godfather *by Francis Ford Coppola*

Francis Ford Coppola's film *The Godfather* is an example of a film that could be used in this question. If you have not seen it, www.imdb.com has a commentary, a very full synopsis and several clips available to view.

(?) Question

Choose a film or television drama that has at its centre a destructive personality.

With reference to appropriate techniques, discuss how the destructive nature of the character is revealed and how this affects your view of the character in the course of the film or television drama.

Answer

1 **Opening paragraph**
At the beginning of the film, the Godfather is portrayed as a destructive character. However, it becomes obvious as the film progresses that it is Michael Corleone who is going to become the truly destructive character, although at the beginning he appears to be striving in the opposite direction.

2 **Concluding paragraph**
These latter scenes, including the sequence of assassinations taking place against the backdrop of a baptism, are especially destructive. This and the subsequent garrotting of Carlo combine to lose Michael any sympathy which his initial predicament might have gained for his character.

3 **Reordering/selecting your material**
The essay would probably revolve round the scenes which reveal the change in Michael – the hospital scene, etc. A lot of the beginning could be omitted. A more in-depth exploration of one of the powerful scenes at the end of the film would illustrate the lengths to which Michael will now go, decreasing the viewer's sympathy.

4 **Central concern(s)**
The central concerns of power and corruption are at the heart of your answer.

5 **Quotation/reference**
As with plays and novels, you could have a stock of short quotations and detailed references you can call on.

6 **Technical features**
You will have been dealing with characterisation throughout, and structural techniques. Filmic techniques will feature in your detailed discussion of a powerful scene. The answer should be based on the changes in Michael's character rather than on a list of particular techniques.

Remember

Don't forget to check your technical accuracy (see page 134).

Before we look at the specific tasks that you have to undertake in order to achieve success in this aspect of your Higher English course, perhaps we ought to look at the value we should be placing on this aspect of communication.

It is highly likely that your future will depend on these skills – possibly more than on your writing abilities. You probably will, in the next year, have to fill in a form or a questionnaire, or create a CV, which will be the start of a process of entry to the next stage of your life – whether in the job market, in an apprenticeship scheme or in a further or higher education course. But that might be just the first step. You might be called for interview. You might have to take part in a group exercise with other candidates. You might be asked to give a presentation demonstrating your knowledge and understanding of the field of work that you wish to enter. All of these scenarios require you to talk, and listen – in fact, probably listen and then talk. Even applying for a part-time or Saturday job could test your verbal communication skills: an S5 student being interviewed for a weekend job in a major chain store was asked to watch a video about one of the products, and then given five minutes to prepare a sales pitch for it. But even if the task is not as daunting as this, at the very least you will have to listen carefully to interview questions, and provide answers that are convincing, confident and useful.

Further on in your career, whatever its nature, you will probably have to convey complex information to peers, fellow workers or your manager, or listen to their comments on your tasks.

As well as the general usefulness of improving these life skills, there is also the necessity to practise them because you have to achieve a certain standard in order to pass your Higher English.

How you are tested in these skills will depend on how your centre decides to gather evidence.

The task

You are required to succeed in at least **one** of the two following tasks:

A **Take part in a group discussion, or discussion-based activity, to which you contribute relevant ideas, opinions, or information, using detailed and complex language. You must take account of the contributions of others and stay focused on the topic or task.**

B **Prepare and present a presentation. The presentation must be detailed and complex in content and must be structured in a clear and relevant way. You must answer questions from the audience at some point in the presentation.**

Your centre will decide how you will be assessed in this activity depending on its knowledge of your teaching group and how best to use time and resources.

Depending on how your centre chooses to assess your skills, either individually or in groups, it may decide to kill two birds with one stone – and save class time – by integrating activities. There are many situations where learning and experience across all the aspects of your course can be integrated.

For example:

- **Issue-based presentation/discussion**
  The same skills and research are required for a piece of discursive writing for your folio, so the material can be used twice – once written and once spoken. But, remember, the spoken version will be different in many ways because it **is** spoken – it is not just reading out your folio piece.
- **Literary text-based presentation/discussion**
  If your class or group has been studying a particular text, then you can share your knowledge with others. This, of course, plays into your work for Critical Essay or Scottish texts.

The following scenarios suggest some of the more common activities that could be used.

The scenario

A

- **Group discussion** functions best when all the members have something useful to contribute, and this depends on each member being prepared for the topic under discussion. If you consider this in the context of a literary text, the whole teaching group is familiar with the text, but each member has a responsibility for a particular aspect. For example, each member of a small group could be responsible for evaluating the contribution of a particular character in a novel, or of a particular technique in a poem. Your ability to follow the discussion and ask other contributors pertinent questions can then be assessed.

- A **discussion-based activity** suggests a slightly different, less formal model, with a looser structure, but with a positive purpose. Examples can be found right across the curriculum – anywhere, in fact, where as a group, or even as a pair, you are asked to 'problem-solve'. In this case preparation is important, but discussion will be based on your prior knowledge of the lesson you have just had, or of the text you have just read, or a topic you have explored on an individual basis. The discussion may develop in unexpected directions – often the most fruitful discoveries are reached by accident – and during it you will have demonstrated that you can present ideas on a complex issue and, by sharing views and opinions, that you can listen carefully.

To underline again the value of these exercises we need only think a little about what the future holds for you.

If you go on to higher education, you will find that in a number of subjects you not only have to use your listening skills in lecture situations, but also use both listening and speaking skills in seminars, or in group work. You may have to put forward an opinion about an issue, or a text, or you may have to explain your solution to a maths problem, or report on practical work you have undertaken.

If you are in competition for a place on a course, or a position of employment, one of the techniques sometimes used by prospective course managers or employers is to set a problem for a group of applicants and see how well they co-operate – do people listen to each other, or do they hog the limelight in competition with others, or do they sit passively, unwilling or unable to contribute to the discussion? No matter how shy you may think you are, and how embarrassed you feel when people turn to look at you, you are going to have to find some mechanism, some strategies, to get around it. And where better to come to terms with these difficulties than in a learning situation, with supportive staff and the chance to try again should you not manage to cope first time?

B

It is highly likely that in your earlier years you will have learned various useful skills, such as PowerPoint presentations, which will have let you practise the mechanics of one type of presentation, but there are many other scenarios that should allow you to demonstrate your skills. Your centre will choose how you should be examined but may adopt one of the following routes:

- A presentation to your teaching group on a topic that you have chosen and researched. The research skills will be exactly the same as those required for one of the essays in your folio – and may indeed be on the same subject. You will also be required to answer questions arising from your presentation. These questions may be from members of your group or from supervising staff. By listening carefully to the questions posed, and providing relevant answers, you will be demonstrating the required listening skills. If your presentation is on the same subject as one of your folio essays, the material you gathered for your essay was probably more extensive than you were able to use within the word limit and that extra material can now give you a wide enough knowledge of your subject to deal with questions arising from your presentation.

- A presentation to a small group, following much the same lines as above, where all of the group can be assessed at the same time. Your listeners have to show, by their questions, that they have listened carefully to you, and your answers to their questions should show that you have listened to, and carefully considered, their questions.

- Your presentation could even be in the form of a discussion between you, as the main speaker, presenting your subject to a listener – possibly a member of staff – who would probe your knowledge of your topic by asking for clarification or expansion of some of your points.

As with the discussion-based activities dealt with in Task A, so there are practical, real-life benefits to being able to present ideas effectively, as required in Task B. Alongside the obvious parallels in further education and employment, think about more everyday situations. In future interactions in real life, such as making complaints to an official body, or defending your position in an interview, you are more likely to be successful if you are able to:

- present your case clearly
- provide back-up information
- listen carefully to the questions and/or replies.

The content

Now that we have considered possible conditions for your discussion/ presentation, it is time to look at the content. If you look back at the language used in the description of the tasks on page 160, you will see that two very important words are 'detailed' and 'complex'.

Just as you wouldn't be asked in the Critical Essay section of the exam paper to 'Tell the story of *The Cone-Gatherers*', you wouldn't expect to succeed in your Speaking and Listening task with a purely narrative presentation of an experience. If you look back at the advice on personal/ reflective writing on pages 10–14, you can see that such an approach would not be successful in writing for your folio either.

If you decide to base your presentation on a personal experience, remember that you have to deal with complex ideas – perhaps the difficulties or challenges you found in processing that experience – in a way that shows mature reflection.

You could also base your presentation on the same material you might have used in a discursive essay, or on your opinions about an issue of importance or on an aspect of literature you have been studying.

You might be tempted to adopt persuasive techniques in your presentation and, in many ways, it is easier to be truly persuasive in speech than it is in writing. Aspects such as tone, gesture and body language (which will be discussed later) can all be effective in promoting an opinion to an audience. A reflective piece can be effective especially if you feel that your experience could be helpful to others in understanding a common situation, or in raising enthusiasm for a worthwhile pastime or project – although that probably goes back to the techniques of persuasion again. As I have said before, nothing you learn in an English class is isolated. Everything you learn or experience feeds into another aspect of your proficiency in English and, from that basis, into your ability to operate effectively and confidently in the world outside school.

Broadly speaking, for a presentation/discussion dealing with opinions, issues or challenges, you should gather material as described on pages 3–9.

For a presentation/discussion dealing with a 'text' (in the broadest sense of the word – literary, film, song, music …) you could look at the Stages outlined in Chapter 5, to give you the material you need.

There are many more scenarios which could be exploited to produce evidence for the skills of Speaking and Listening. For example, you could use an entertainment format, such as a chat show or a question time set-up. Or you could set up a planning meeting for a possible joint project for your group. An important thing to remember, however, is that the content must be '**detailed and complex**'.

Delivery

There are two features to mention under this heading. The first is that the language should be of a **complex nature, detailed and appropriate for your audience**. As your audience is likely to be within your school/college, it follows that using too much slang is likely to be unacceptable, and that while a lively discussion might well be the result of an excellent presentation, one that includes personal insults and inappropriate terminology (such as swearing) will be unacceptable.

A second feature of your delivery is important – however good your research, however well organised your thoughts, however important your conclusion, your duty to your audience is to communicate and in order to communicate you have **to be heard**. If your voice is too soft, or you speak too quickly, or you mumble, your audience will not hear what you have to say and **you cannot pass**. You will not have demonstrated that 'effective communication is achieved'.

This is exactly the same kind of challenge that you were alerted to with respect to the writing 'Hints & tips' on page 2.

Again, the context in which you make your presentation, or take part in discussion, will lead to a variation in demand. If you are speaking to a small group round a table, where you can all see each other, then volume, or projection, will be less important. But clarity is still paramount. If the rest of the group cannot hear you properly, they will be unable to ask sensible questions, with the result that you won't succeed in achieving your target and the rest of the group won't be able to fulfil the listening requirement.

If your presentation is to a larger group, then volume, or projection, becomes more important. There are a few tips that help the audience to hear you more easily. The first, but not most obvious thing, is that they can see you – if the audience can see the face of the person talking, they actually hear them better. They seem to pick up clues from the shape of the mouth, from the slight movements that normally signal the end of sentences – even from the intake of breath which heralds a new topic. So:

- stand so that those at the back can see you
- try to find a place where the lighting in the room is good, so that your face can be seen
- make sure your hair doesn't prevent the audience from seeing your mouth and eyes
- if you are using a screen to show illustrations or to flag up headings, do not have the screen directly behind you; if you do then you will appear in silhouette and your face will be in the dark
- don't keep looking down at your notes.

It should be obvious from the above list that **reading your presentation** means that it is difficult for people to see your face and get clues from your facial expression. To misquote Hamlet: 'To read or not to read, that is the question.' And the answer, very definitely, is **not to read**. This may be difficult to begin with, but practice always helps. Try the following to get your thoughts into some sort of order. (You can abandon this structure once you are confident about your material.)

1 Make headings for your talk, in the same way as you may produce a topic sentence at the beginning of each paragraph in a writing task.

2 Then make two or three sub-headings under each main one. But avoid the temptation to fill in any more than that.

3 You 'fill in' as you deliver your **spoken** presentation, and the words come out of your knowledge of the topic you are dealing with. You can practise filling in under each heading by speaking to yourself, or the mirror, or the dog, but do it **without writing anything down**.

4 Practise it again. The words will not be exactly the same – something may have been left out or something more important inserted, but it will still cover the point and it will sound like your **speaking** 'voice', not your **reading** one.

5 You may wish to make a list of quotations you want to use – perhaps what a politician has said about your topic, or a what a character in a play you are discussing has said at a crucial moment. Obviously, you can read those out, but they shouldn't be too long, nor should there be too many of them.

Hints & tips

Tone can give a clue to your audience: serious, sarcastic, sad, enthusiastic — these are just a few examples. In an oral presentation there is less likely to be a misunderstanding of content, as the tone does not have to be guessed from the writing.

Hints & tips

You can provide yourself with some props, just in case you lose the thread of your talk, or you feel nervous at the start.

1 You could write out your opening sentences and try to memorise them, but having them in your notes will give you confidence at the start.

2 You could write a link between one topic/paragraph and the next, so that if you get lost you can move on to the next point.

3 You could write out the last few sentences of your conclusion. Again, you can try to memorise them, so that you don't have to read them, but the words will be there if you need them, and if you have a good conclusion it can let you finish on a high, even if some of the bits in between have been a bit shaky.

All these things apply no matter what size your audience is — whether it's twenty people or one, you must know where you are going and how you want to reach your goal of communicating to your listener(s) something of importance about your topic.

Your notes

Your notes should provide a skeleton for your talk. You then put the flesh on in real time for your audience. Aim to keep your notes as short as possible, so that there is no temptation for you to read at length.

How you make your notes depends very much on the type of thought processes that suit you. And how you record them – on paper, on cards, on slides – will depend on what sort of presentation you are giving and in what kind of scenario.

For many people, the following kind of structure can be useful (remember, once you have practised and are confident about your material you can abandon this structure for a more relaxed and spontaneous approach):

Opening sentences: 100 words maximum.

First main heading:
- Point (a)
- Point (b)
- Point (c)
- Link sentence: 'Adding to … I now want to let you see …' OR, 'On the other hand, there is the matter of …'

Second main heading:
- Point (a)
- Point (b)
- Link …

Third main heading:
- Point (a)
- Point (b)
- **Conclusion**: finishing with perhaps a prepared sentence or two (again, 100 words maximum).

If you want to include quotations, perhaps the best place would be in another column beside the points they are illustrating, so that you can find them without any fuss.

There are, of course, other possibilities such as a table or a spatial diagram or slides.

Note: if you do decide to illustrate your talk with slides (which may act as your 'notes'), avoid the temptation to read out what is there (your audience can read, after all) and instead concentrate on expanding the headings on the slides with your knowledge of your subject in an interesting way.

Length

There is no prescribed length for this task: a discussion group could last for many minutes or even hours. A problem-solving task, or a task with an 'end product', could take an unpredictable amount of time; but in this case, where we are dealing with classroom parameters, unlimited time is not available. Each centre will decide what length of time it feels is appropriate for its students and the specification of the tasks they have been given. No maximum or minimum is prescribed. If, however, we look at an average piece of discursive writing of, say 1100 words, it would take about seven minutes to read it out loud. This probably suggests that to deal with a complex subject in a presentation or as a starter for a discussion you would probably need four or five minutes, but that would only be a guide. It would depend on how you were going to introduce your subject, and in what detail you were going to develop it. Questions from your listener(s) might involve you in further interesting contributions to your topic.

Non-verbal features

As mentioned above on page 165, oral presentation allows a wide range of immediately effective techniques to emphasis your meaning and line of argument.

These might include facial expression, emphasis, gesture, eye contact, etc.

- **Facial expression** can give clues as to what emotion is behind a particular part of your presentation. For example, is this part serious or funny, or surprising, or questionable?
- **Eye contact** helps to make a connection between you and your audience, and has the additional virtue of keeping your head up so that your face and expression can be seen. It is very likely to be the main non-verbal feature in group discussion, where gesture and body language are less necessary to make a point.
- **Gesture** does not mean that you have to stomp up and down flailing your arms (although that might be effective in some instances) – often it is simply something like spreading your hands to suggest that there is a question to be considered, or simply straightening up when you come to a really important point, or, indeed, pointing to emphasise an aspect of a phrase you have just used, or perhaps repeated. But on other occasions it could be as simple as nodding to acknowledge a question.
- **Body language** may consist of something as simple as adopting a confident stance or leaning forward in a group situation to make your point. Your head inclined always downwards to the floor or your notes, or leaning back in your chair when listening, does not promote confidence in either the speaker or the listeners.

Listening

It is obvious that listening is an integral part of all that has been dealt with already, but as it is a skill that has to be assessed, we should perhaps try to pin down what a helpful and effective listener does.

First of all, **active listening** requires concentration and memory. This is not a passive activity. As with **active reading** (see page 143), active listening possibly needs a few notes jotted down to remind you of the main points of what you are listening to. The presenter is not the only one working; your contribution is going to be required later.

Your job is to ask relevant questions or make useful comments at the end of the presentation. You might:

- ask for clarification of a point that seemed a little confused; this helps the presenter by giving them another chance to relay the information in an effective way
- ask for an expansion of a point that particularly interested you; again, this helps the presenter to add extra detail to the topic
- challenge (politely) the standpoint of the presenter by putting forward a relevant alternative opinion on the topic. This (generally) can be seen as helpful in that more evidence can be brought in to illuminate the argument.

In a presentation at the start of a small group discussion, it is possible that all members of the group have knowledge of the subject and can, by putting forward appropriate questions and ideas, add, broaden or refine their joint knowledge to the benefit of the whole group.

In a group discussion where there is no formal 'opening presentation', there has to be some method of organising the proceedings so that each person can contribute in response to a stimulus of some sort – it could be the stimulus is a question about the central concerns of a text they have all studied. Listening carefully and responding relevantly by expansion or with other ideas on the topic should lead to all members of the group demonstrating their skill in Listening, and cumulatively they may also have demonstrated their skill in Speaking.

Remember

In all these activities, you have to deal with ideas and opinions of some complexity and detail. 'The Rules of Tiddlywinks' is unlikely to cut it!

Acknowledgements

Marking information and assessment overview (p.iv), information on marking style (p.27) and guidance on technical accuracy (p.2, p.24, p.134) are adapted from SQA material copyright © Scottish Qualifications Authority. Reproduced by permission of SQA.

Jon Absalom: Extracts from 'The truth about life as a househusband' from *The Guardian* (27 October 2005) © Guardian News and Media Ltd. Reprinted with permission.

Vicky Allan: Extract from 'All kids want for Christmas is technology' from the *Sunday Herald*, (15 December 2013). Reprinted with permission of Sunday Herald.

Ian Bell: Extracts from 'Divided we fall' from the *Sunday Herald* (29 December 2013) and 'Is Twitter dumbing us down?' from the *Sunday Herald* (5 January 2014). Reprinted with permission of Sunday Herald.

Libby Brooks: Extract from 'So you want them to be happy?' from *The Guardian* (16 September 2006) © Guardian News and Media Ltd. Reprinted with permission.

Joshua Constine: Extract from 'You should use Twitter because it makes everyone as smart as anyone' (post on Twitter) from *www.techcrunch.com* (11 November, 2013).

Rachel Cooke: Extract from 'To bring girls into sport, get rid of old ideas about "femininity"' from *The Observer* (22 February 2014) © Guardian News and Media Ltd. Reprinted with permission.

Carol Ann Duffy: 'Originally' from *The Other Country*, 1990. Published by Picador, 2009. Copyright © Carol Ann Duffy. 'Mrs Midas' from *The World's Wife* (Picador, 2010). Published by Picador, 1999. Copyright © Carol Ann Duffy. Both reproduced by permission of the author c/o Rogers, Coleridge & White Ltd., 20 Powis Mews, London W11 1JN.

Terry Eagleton: Extract from 'I am not connected' from *Prospect Magazine* (July 2013). Reprinted with permission.

Lawrence Ferlinghetti: Extract from 'The Kiss – Short Story on a Painting of Gustav Klimt'. From ENDLESS LIFE, copyright © 1976 by Lawrence Ferlinghetti. Reprinted by permission of New Directions Publishing Corp.

Kevin Fong: Extract from '*Voyager 1* keeps on trucking' from *The Observer* (24 December 2017) © Guardian News and Media Ltd. Reprinted with permission.

Jonathan Freedland: Extract from 'Food banks or dignity: is that the choice we offer the hungry?' from *The Guardian* (21 February 2014) © Guardian News and Media Ltd. Reprinted with permission.

Suzanne Goldenberg: Extract from 'Marine mining: Underwater gold rush sparks fears of ocean catastrophe' from *The Observer* (2 March 2014) © Guardian News and Media Ltd. Reprinted with permission.

Lewis Grassic Gibbon: Extracts from *Sunset Song* (Jarrold Publishing, 1932). Public domain.

Gwen Harwood: 'Surburban Sonnet' from *Selected Poems* (Penguin Australia, 2001).

Robin Jenkins: Extracts from *The Cone-Gatherers* (1955; Canongate Books, 2004) © Canongate Books, 1955. Reprinted with permission.

India Knight: Extract from 'Oh do try to be more feminine, you sporting goddesses' from *The Times* (23 February 2014), The Sunday Times. Reprinted with permission.

Philip Larkin: Extract from 'Church Going' from *Philip Larkin: Collected Poems* (Faber & Faber, 1990). © Philip Larkin. Reprinted with permission of Faber & Faber.

John McGrath: Extract from *The Cheviot, the Stag and the Black, Black Oil* (Methuen Drama, 1981). Reproduced by permission of Bloomsbury Publishing plc.

Joanna Moorehead: Extract from 'The joys of a 21st century childhood' from *The Independent*, (13 September 2006) The Independent. Reprinted with permission.

Sylvia Patterson: Extract from 'Swallow your pride and save our fish' from *The Herald (Glasgow)*, (13 June 2009). The Herald.

Iain Crichton Smith: Extract from *Home* from *The Red Door: The Complete English Short Stories, 1949–76* (Birlinn, 2001). © Birlinn. Reproduced with permission of the Licensor through PLSclear.

David Stephen: Extract from 'Seven swans' from *String Lug the Fox* (Lutterworth Press, 1950). © Lutterworth Press. Reprinted with permission.

Robert Louis Stevenson: Extracts from *The Strange Case of Doctor Jekyll and Mr Hyde* (Longmans, Green & Co, 1886). Public domain.

Every effort has been made to trace all copyright holders, but if any have been inadvertently overlooked the Publishers will be pleased to make the necessary arrangements at the first opportunity.